Novelist as a

Vocation

Also by Haruki Murakami

FICTION

1Q84
After Dark
After the Quake
Blind Willow, Sleeping Woman
Colorless Tsukuru Tazaki and His Years of Pilgrimage
Dance Dance Dance
The Elephant Vanishes
First Person Singular
Hard-Boiled Wonderland and the End of the World
Kafka on the Shore
Killing Commendatore
Norwegian Wood
South of the Border, West of the Sun
Sputnik Sweetheart
The Strange Library
A Wild Sheep Chase
Wind/Pinball
The Wind-Up Bird Chronicle

NONFICTION

Absolutely on Music (with Seiji Ozawa)
Underground: The Tokyo Gas Attack and the Japanese Psyche
What I Talk About When I Talk About Running: A Memoir
Murakami T

Haruki Murakami

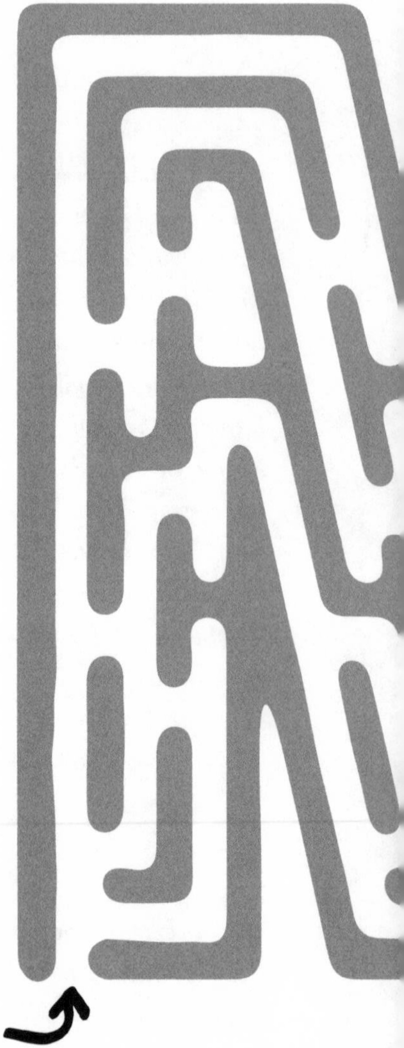

Novelist as a

Vocation

Translated from the Japanese by Philip Gabriel and Ted Goossen

Alfred A. Knopf *New York* 2022

THIS IS A BORZOI BOOK
PUBLISHED BY ALFRED A. KNOPF

www.aaknopf.com

Knopf, Borzoi Books, and the colophon are registered
trademarks of Penguin Random House LLC.

Library of Congress Cataloging-in-Publication Data
Names: Murakami, Haruki, 1949- author. | Gabriel, Philip, 1953- translator. |
    Goossen, Ted, translator.
Title: Novelist as a vocation / Haruki Murakami ; translated from the Japanese
    by Philip Gabriel and Ted Goossen.
Other titles: Shokugyåo to shite no shåosetsuka. English
Description: First edition. | New York : Alfred A. Knopf, 2022. | "This is a Borzoi book"
Identifiers: LCCN 2022021694| ISBN 9780451494641 (hardcover) |
    ISBN 9781101974537 (trade paperback) | ISBN 9780451494658 (ebook)
Subjects: | LCGFT: Essays.
Classification: LCC PL856.U673 S5613 2022 | DDC 895.64/5 23/eng/20220—dc06
LC record available at https://lccn.loc.gov/2022021694

Jacket illustration by Chip Kidd, based on an image by Milos Kojadinovic / Alamy
Jacket design by Chip Kidd

Manufactured in the United States of America
First Edition

CONTENTS

FOREWORD

I'm not exactly sure when I began writing the series of essays collected in this volume, but I think it was around 2010.

One thing I need to mention is that this book was published in Japan in 2015, so there is a seven-year time lag between that and the present 2022 English translation. I'd like you to be aware of this. During these past seven years we've experienced all kinds of crucial events, including the Corona pandemic, and wars breaking out around the world. These circumstances have forced us to make some significant changes in our lives. These essays, though, do not reflect those changes, or the individual changes I've experienced myself. They are simply my thoughts and feelings as of 2015.

———

FOR A LONG TIME I've been wanting to say something about my writing novels, and being a novelist for so long; so in between other work I started, bit by bit, jotting down my thoughts, and organizing them by topic. I didn't write these essays, then, at the request of a publisher, but, rather, on my own initiative, something I wrote for my own sake.

The first several chapters I wrote in my usual style—like how I'm writing here—but when I reread them the flow of the writing seemed stiff and kind of shrill, and it just didn't sit well with me. So I tried writing as if I were directly talking to people, and that way it felt easier to write (speak) more smoothly and honestly; and decided to consolidate the whole thing as if I were writing a speech. I pictured myself speaking in a small hall to maybe thirty or forty people, and rewrote the essays in the more intimate tone you'd expect in that kind of setting. Though I never actually had the opportunity to read these essays as talks in front of anyone.

Why not? First of all, I feel a bit embarrassed about talking about myself, and about the process of me writing novels, so directly and openly. I have a pretty strong desire not to try to explain my novels to others. Talking about my own works always comes off sounding kind of apologetic, or boastful, or as if I'm trying to justify myself. Even if I don't want to sound that way, it still leaves that impression.

Well, I imagine that someday I might have the chance to talk about this in public, but it might be a little early for it now. Maybe when I'm a bit older. Thinking this, I tossed the pages I'd written into a drawer. From time to time I'd take them out and rework parts of the manuscript. The situation surrounding me—my personal circumstances, societal circumstances—was gradually changing, as was my way of thinking and feeling about things. In that sense the version I wrote in the beginning and the final version here are very different in feeling and tone. Still, my fundamental stance and way of thinking have hardly changed at all. It almost makes me feel like I've been saying the same things from the time I debuted down to today. When I read what I said over thirty years ago I'm surprised, thinking, "Wow, it's almost exactly what I'm saying now!"

So I think what's collected here are things I've been writing and saying over and over (though the form may have gradually changed over time). Many readers might think, "Hey, haven't I read that somewhere before?" and if you're one of them I ask your indulgence. Another motivation for publishing these "records of undelivered speeches" was a desire to systematically gather all the things I've said in different places. I'd be pleased if readers would take these as a comprehensive look (at the present time) of my views on writing novels.

The first half of this book was serialized in the magazine *Monkey Business*. Motoyuki Shibata started this new magazine in 2008 (which was to be a new type of more intimate literary journal) and asked me if I'd write something for it. I agreed, and gave him a short story, one I'd just happened to have finished, and a thought occurred to me and I told him, "You know, I have these personal speeches I've written. If you have space, could you serialize them?"

That's how the first six chapters came to be serialized in each monthly issue of *Monkey Business*. An easy task, since all I had to do was turn over for every issue something I already had lying dormant in my drawer. In all there are eleven chapters, the first six, as I've said, serialized in the magazine, the last five written especially for this book.

I imagine this book will be taken as *autobiographical essays*, but they weren't originally written with that in mind. What I was after was to write, in the most concrete and practical way, about the path I've followed as a novelist, and the ideas and thoughts I've had in the process. That said, writing novels is nothing less than expressing yourself, so talking about the process of writing means you inevitably have to talk about yourself.

Truthfully, I have no idea if this book could serve as a guidebook or introduction to help those hoping to write novels. What I mean is, I'm the kind of person with a very individual way of thinking, and I don't know how far you can generalize about or apply my way of writing and living. I know hardly any other writers, so I don't know how they write, and I can't make comparisons. For me, this is the only way I can write, so that's how I do it. I'm certainly not advocating this as the best way to write novels. You might be able to apply some things in my methods, but others might not work so well. It goes without saying, but if you take a hundred novelists you'll find a hundred different ways of writing novels. I hope that each of you grasps that and comes to your own conclusions about any applications.

One thing I do want you to understand is that I am, when all is said and done, a *very ordinary person*. I do think I have some innate ability to write novels (if I didn't, I wouldn't have been able to write novels all these many years). But that aside, if I do say so myself, I'm the type of ordinary guy you'll find anywhere. Not the type to stand out when I stroll around town, the type who's always shown to the worst tables at restaurants. I doubt that if I didn't write novels, anyone would ever have noticed me. I would have just lived out an ordinary, nondescript life in a totally ordinary way. In my daily life I'm hardly ever conscious of myself as writer.

But since I do happen to have a bit of ability to write novels, and have had some good luck on my side, plus a stubborn streak (or, to put it more nicely, a consistency) that's proved helpful, I've been able, over thirty-five years, to write novels as a profession. To this day it continues to amaze me. It really does. What I've wanted to talk about in this book is that very sense of amazement, about the strong desire (or will, you might say) to hold onto the purity of that feeling of amazement. Perhaps the past thirty-five years of my life have been the ardent pursuit to maintain that sense of amazement. It certainly feels that way.

The last thing I'd like to note is that I'm not the kind of person who is very good at thinking things out purely using my mind. I'm not that good at logical argument or abstract thought. The only way I can think about things in any kind of order is by putting them in writing. Physically moving my hand as I write, rereading what I write, over and over, and closely reworking it—only then am I finally able to gather my thoughts and grasp them like other people do. Because of this, through writing over time what's been gathered in this volume, and rewriting it over and over, I've been able to think more systematically and take a broader view of myself, a novelist, and myself being a novelist.

I wonder, then, how useful this somewhat self-indulgent, personal writing here—less message than record of a personal thought process—will prove to the reader. If it does turn out to be even a little useful in a practical way, I would be very pleased.

(Originally written in June 2015; updated in June 2022)

Novelist as a

Vocation

Are Novelists Broad-minded?

TALKING ABOUT NOVELS strikes me as too broad and amorphous a topic to get the ball rolling, so I will start by addressing something more specific: novelists. They are concrete and visible, and therefore easier to deal with.

There are exceptions, of course, but from what I have seen, most novelists aren't what one would call amiable and fair-minded. Neither are they what would normally be considered good role models: their dispositions tend to be idiosyncratic and their lifestyles and general behavior frankly odd. Almost all (my guess is 92 percent, including yours truly) live under the unspoken assumption that "my way is right, while virtually all other writers are wrong." I doubt that many of us would want to have much contact with such people, whether as neighbors or—heaven forbid—as friends.

When I hear that two writers are good buddies, I tend to take it with a grain of salt. Sure, I think, those things can happen, but a truly intimate friendship of that sort can't last very long. Writers are basically an egoistic breed, proud and highly competitive. Put two of them in the same room and the result, more likely than not, will be a disappointment. Believe me, I have been in that situation a number of times myself.

One famous example was the 1922 dinner party in Paris that brought together Marcel Proust and James Joyce. They were seated close to each other, and everyone there held their breath to hear what those towering figures of twentieth-century literature would say. Yet in the end everyone's expectations were dashed, for the two barely spoke to each other. I imagine their self-regard was just too great a hurdle to overcome.

Nevertheless, if the conversation shifts to exclusionary attitudes—simply put, the territorial instinct—among professional groups, it strikes me that few, if any, tribes are as generous and welcoming as novelists. Indeed, I think that may be one of the very few virtues novelists possess.

Let me be a little more specific.

Suppose that a novelist blessed with a good voice makes his or her debut as a singer. Or a novelist with an aptitude for art exhibits paintings. Without a doubt, they would be met with resistance, even ridicule. The critics would go to town. "Stick to what you know!" some would sneer. Others would crow, "An amateurish display, lacking in skill or talent." Professional singers and artists would likely turn a cold shoulder. Comments might even grow malicious. In any case, a "Welcome to the club!" sort of greeting would be rare on either front. Should a warm reception be proffered, it would doubtless be on a very limited scale in a very restricted venue.

Alongside my own fiction, I have been publishing translations of American literature for thirty years, yet in the beginning (and possibly even now) I was raked over the coals by professionals in the field for doing so. "Literary translation is not for mere amateurs," shouted a chorus of voices. "Writers who try their hand at translation are just a nuisance."

Similarly, when I published *Underground*, I was met with harsh criticism from the ranks of professional nonfiction writers: "a display of ignorance of the basic rules of nonfiction"; "a tearjerker of the first order"; "the work of a dilettante." I had not attempted to write nonfiction per se; rather, I had attempted to produce a work unbeholden to any genre that handled "nonfictional" material. Nevertheless, I had stepped on the tails of the tigers who guard the sacred sanctuary of nonfiction, and they were angry. I had not known that they existed, or that there were hard-and-fast rules that governed such writing, so at first I was completely bewildered.

As my experience suggests, specialists in a given field tend to frown on those who, for whatever reason, stray onto their turf. Like the white blood cells that protect our bodies from foreign invaders, they repel all "alien" forces. Those who proceed undaunted may find, in the end, that the authorities have relented, and that their admittance has been tacitly approved . . . but in the beginning at least the road is bound to be rocky. The narrower and more specialized the field, I have found, the prouder the authorities tend to be and the stronger their antipathy to outsiders.

B u t   w h a t   o f the opposite case, when singers or artists or translators or nonfiction writers turn out a novel? Do novelists make a sour face? From my experience, no. To the contrary, we tend to look upon the results positively, and even encourage their authors. Certainly I have never witnessed an established novelist dismiss a first-timer with an angry "What the hell do you think you're doing?!" Nor have I heard of newcomers being insulted or ridiculed or maliciously tripped up by their more experienced brethren. Instead, it is likely that curious senior writers will invite them to discuss their work and possibly offer them advice and encouragement.

This is not to say, of course, that novelists do not say negative things about first novels in private, but they do that about one another's works all the time, too: indeed, such criticisms are the norm in all workplaces and bear no relation to the desire to repel outside invaders. Novelists are riddled with faults, but that is not one of them: as a rule, they are magnanimous with those who step onto their turf, and treat them generously.

Why should that be so?

I think I have a pretty good idea. The thing that makes novels different is that practically anybody can write one if they put their mind to it. A pianist or a ballerina has to go through a process of severe, intensive training from childhood until, finally, they are able to make their debut; an artist has to be equipped with at least a modicum of knowledge and foundational skills, not to mention a full set of tools and other materials. Becoming a mountain climber requires an inordinate amount of physical strength, training, and courage.

An aspiring novelist, by contrast, needs only the basic ability to write (most people have that), a ballpoint pen, a pad of paper, and the capacity to make up a story to turn out something resembling a novel—whether they have received any specialized training is quite beside the point. There is no need to study literature at the university level. It's fine if you've studied creative writing, but just as fine if you haven't.

It's possible for a first-timer to produce a fine novel if he or she is blessed with just a little talent. When I started, for example, I had zero training. True, I had majored in drama and film in university, but times being what they were—it was the late 1960s—I had seldom attended class. Instead, I grew long hair and a scruffy beard and hung around in clothes that were less than clean. I had no special plans to become a writer, never even tried to scribble something down for practice, until one day the bug suddenly bit me and I wrote my first novel (if you want to call it that), *Hear the Wind Sing*, which ended up winning a literary magazine's prize for new writers. I went on to become a professional writer without ever having had to study the craft. "Is this really all right?" I asked myself, shaking my head in wonder. It all seemed way too easy.

This may anger some people. I can hear them squawking, "What the hell do you know about literature?" I'm just trying to tell it like it really is. People can theorize all they want, but when you get right down to it, the novel's form is extremely broad. Indeed, that very breadth is what helps to generate its amazing, down-to-earth vitality. From where I stand, the statement "Anyone can write a novel" is not slander, but praise.

In short, the world of the novelist is like a professional wrestling ring that welcomes anyone who feels like taking a crack at it. The gap between the ropes is big enough to pass through, and a step is provided to make your entrance easier. The ring is spacious. No security men block your way, and the referee doesn't bark at you to leave. The wrestlers who are already there—the established novelists, in other words—are at the very least resigned to your presence: "No worries—come on up and take your best shot" is their attitude. The ring is—how shall I put this?—an airy, easy, accommodating, altogether laid-back environment.

While entering the ring may be easy, however, remaining there for long is hard. We novelists are of course aware of this. It's not that difficult to write a novel, maybe even two. But it's another thing altogether to keep producing, to live off one's writing, to survive. That's a Herculean task. It's fair to say not many are up to it. To accomplish it, one needs, well, a special something. Talent is important, of course, and backbone. Like so many things in life, luck and fate play a big role, too. But there is something else that is needed, a kind of qualification. Some have it and some don't. Some possess it from birth while others struggle mightily to acquire it.

Not very much is known about this qualification—indeed, it is seldom addressed in public. The reason, for the most part, is that it is virtually impossible to visualize or put into words. Yet novelists are keenly aware of its importance and of how necessary it is to sustain their craft—they can feel it in their bones.

I think this is why novelists tend to be so generous to outsiders who step up through the ropes to make their novelistic debuts. "Come on in," some will say, while others seem to take no notice of the new kid in the ring. When the newcomer is unceremoniously tossed out or steps down voluntarily (most will fall into one of these two categories), the old-timers will say "Too bad, kid," or "Take care of yourself." If someone manages to stick it out for the long term, on the other hand, those novelists gain well-earned respect. This respect will be given rightly and properly (or so I would like to believe).

Another reason novelists can be so magnanimous is that they understand literary business is not a zero-sum game. In other words, the fact that a new writer has appeared in the ring almost never means someone already there will have to step down. On the surface, at least, that kind of thing doesn't happen. In that sense, the world of writers and the world of professional athletes are diametrically opposed. In pro sports, when a rookie makes the team, an old-timer or another new player who has failed to impress is either given their walking papers or moved to the far end of the bench. No parallel exists in the literary world. In the same vein, when a new novel sells a hundred thousand copies, that total isn't subtracted from the total sales of other works. To the contrary, a runaway bestseller by a new writer can give the whole publishing industry a boost.

Nevertheless, if one takes the long view, a fitting kind of natural selection is in operation. The ring may be spacious, but there still appears to be an optimal number of writers inside it. Such, at least, is my impression.

I HAVE BEEN getting by one way or another as a professional novelist for over thirty-five years, as of 2015, when I wrote this. In short, I have been in the ring all that time—"living by the pen," to use the old term. This, I guess, can be regarded as a real accomplishment in the narrow sense of the word.

I have seen the debuts of a great many new writers during that time. Many have been praised to the skies for their works. They have been toasted by the critics, awarded various literary prizes, talked about by the public, and have sold lots of books. Bright hopes have been held out for their futures. In other words, they have stepped up into the ring bathed in the spotlights, their theme music rising around them.

Yet how many of those budding writers who debuted twenty or thirty years ago are active as novelists today? Not many. Only a very few, to be more precise. The rest have quietly slipped from the ring. In many, perhaps the majority of, cases, they have gravitated to other fields, having grown tired of novel writing; or perhaps they simply found it too much trouble. And those first novels that received so much attention? One would probably have a hard time locating them in bookstores today. Although the potential number of novelists may be limitless, the amount of shelf space is most certainly finite!

The way I see it, people with brilliant minds are not particularly well suited to writing novels. Of course some degree of intelligence and education and overall knowledge is necessary to turn one out. I myself am not entirely lacking in those areas. At least I think so. Probably. But if someone were to ask me point-blank "Do you really think you're smart enough?" I'd have a hard time sounding confident.

In my considered opinion, anyone with a quick mind or an inordinately rich store of knowledge is unlikely to become a novelist. That is because the writing of a novel, or the telling of a story, is an activity that takes place at a slow pace—in low gear, so to speak. Faster than walking, let's say, but slower than riding a bicycle. The basic speed of a person's mental processes may make it possible to work at that rate, or it may not.

For the most part, novelists are trying to convert something present in their consciousness into a story. Yet there is an inevitable gap between the preexisting original and the new shape it is spawning. That creates a dynamic the novelist can use as a kind of lever in the fashioning of his narrative. This is quite a roundabout way to do things, and it takes a great deal of time.

Someone whose message is clearly formed has no need to go through the many steps it would take to transpose that message into a story. All he has to do is put it directly into words—it's much faster and can be easily communicated to an audience. A message or concept that might take six months to turn into a novel can thus be fully developed in a mere three days. Or in ten minutes, if the writer has a microphone and can spit it out as it comes to him. Quick thinkers are capable of that kind of thing. The listener will slap his knee and marvel, "Why didn't I think of that?!" In the final analysis, that's what being smart is really all about.

In the same vein, it is unnecessary for someone with a wealth of knowledge to drag out a fuzzy, dubious container like the novel for his purposes. No need for him to set up an imaginary time and place from scratch. All he has to do is rationally organize and then put into words the information he has on hand to wow his audience.

It is for these reasons, I think, that so many critics have trouble understanding—or, if they can understand at all, effectively verbalizing or theorizing that understanding—a *certain type* of novel or story. Such critics are generally smarter than the novelists whose works they analyze, which means their brains move at a more rapid speed. They may not be able to adjust to the slower vehicle that is the novel. As a result, they "translate" the pace of the text into the faster pace that is natural to them and then construct their critique in line with their version. This approach fits certain texts, but not all. It may work well in some cases but fail in others. It is especially problematic when the text under discussion is not just "slow" but operates at multiple levels with significant complexity. In such cases, their so-called translation twists and distorts the original.

At any rate, I have witnessed a great many intelligent and quick-minded people—many hailing from fields other than literature—head off to new destinations after writing a novel or two. In a great many cases, their novels were brilliant and well written. A few of them have even broken new ground. Yet a scant few of those authors have remained in the ring. In fact, it seems to me that they got a taste of the novelist's vocation and then made a quick exit.

Another reason why so few stick it out is that someone with a fair amount of literary talent may have a single novel in them that they can roll out fairly easily, but no more. Or someone who is highly intelligent fails to find the payoff they anticipated. Such writers, after turning out one or two novels, may say, "Okay, now I get it," shrug their shoulders, and move on to something that will use their time and energy more efficiently.

I understand these feelings. Novel writing is indeed a most inefficient undertaking, consisting of repeating "for instance" over and over. Say there is a personal theme you wish to develop. So you transpose it into a different context. "For instance, it could be like this," you say. That transposition or paraphrase, however, is not complete: it has parts that are unclear and fuzzy. So you start a new section that basically says, "Let me give you another 'for instance.' " It can go on and on like that, a chain of paraphrased "for instances" that never ends. It's like one of those Russian dolls that you open again and again, always to find still another, smaller doll inside. Could there be more circuitous, inefficient work than this? If a theme could be voiced clearly and rationally from the outset, then there would be no need for this incessant round of "for instances." An extreme way of putting it is that novelists might be defined as a breed who feel the need, in spite of everything, to do that which is unnecessary.

Yet the novelist will claim that truth and reality are entrenched in precisely such unnecessary, roundabout places. I know it may sound pretentious, but it is in this belief that the novelist plies his craft. Thus it is natural that we find, on the one hand, people who believe that there is no need for novels and, on the other, those who maintain that novels are absolutely necessary. It all depends on the time span you adopt and the type of framework through which you view things. More precisely, our world is constructed in a multi-layered way, so that the realm of the roundabout and the inefficient is in fact the flip side of that which is clever and efficient. If one or the other is missing (or if one is dominated by the other), then the world is distorted as a result.

WRITING NOVELS IS, to my way of thinking, basically a very uncool enterprise. I see hardly anything chic or stylish about it. Novelists sit cloistered in their rooms, intently fiddling with words, batting around one possibility after another. They may scratch their heads an entire day to improve the quality of a single line by a tiny bit. No one applauds, or says "Well done," or pats them on the back. Sitting there alone, they look over what they've accomplished and quietly nod to themselves. It may be that later, when the novel comes out, not a single reader will notice the improvement they made that day. That is what novel writing is really all about. It is time-consuming, tedious work.

I CAN'T HELP thinking that novelists share something in common with those who spend a year or more assembling miniature boats in bottles with long tweezers. I couldn't possibly do that—my fingertips aren't that dexterous—but on some essential level what I do and what they do seem quite similar. We spend our time behind closed doors doing the most intricate type of operations, day after day after day. The process is virtually endless. If you aren't built for that sort of work and can't shrug off all that it entails, there's no way you'll keep it up over the long haul.

I remember reading a book when I was a boy about two men who travel to learn what there is to know about Mount Fuji. Neither of them has ever seen Fuji before. The smarter of the two men sizes up the mountain from several vantage points at the foot of its slopes. Then he says, "So this is the famous Fuji-san. Now I see what makes it so special," and heads back home, satisfied. His way is efficient. And fast. The less intelligent man can't figure it out like that, so he stays behind to climb the mountain all the way to its summit. This takes a lot of time and effort. By the end he has used up all his strength and is completely pooped. "So that's Mount Fuji, huh?" he thinks. Finally, he has understood it, or perhaps grasped its essence at a less conscious level.

Novelists (at least most of them) tend to be more like the second man—in other words, the stupider guy. They are the type who has to climb to the top to understand Mount Fuji. Or perhaps it is in their nature to climb the mountain over and over without ever figuring it out; or, again, to find that the more times they climb it, the less they understand. So much for efficiency! Whichever the case, it's the sort of thing a smart person could never stand doing.

This is why a novelist is not alarmed when someone from another field writes a critically and publicly acclaimed novel, even if it goes on to become a bestseller. They do not feel threatened. Or (I think) angry. They know that the chances are small that such a writer will go on to a long career. Smart people work at their own special pace, intellectuals at theirs and scholars at theirs. None of these, however, is a pace suited to writing novels over the long term.

Of course there are smart people among the ranks of established authors. Some others are highly intelligent. That intelligence, however, is more than the normal kind—it is also a *novelistic intelligence*. Even in such cases, my experience has indicated that there is a limit—in simple terms, a novelist's best-before date, which, in my estimation, is about ten years—to how far that can take you. After that point, intelligence has to be replaced by some larger, more enduring gift. Put another way, the razor's edge must give way to the hatchet's edge, which in turn must be superseded by the axe's edge. Any novelist who is able to navigate those stages successfully is elevated—in all likelihood becoming a literary figure whose work transcends the times. Those who can't make these adjustments, however, tend to see their stars fade or disappear altogether. Or they will find a spot to settle down, where they can live a more comfortable and leisurely life in a place amenable to smart people.

A novelist, however, sees the idea of "a leisurely life" as practically synonymous with "the waning of one's creativity." For novelists are like certain types of fish. If they don't keep swimming forward, they die.

THIS IS WHY I hold all those who persist in writing novels over many years without getting fed up—in other words, my colleagues—in such high esteem. Of course my personal likes and dislikes cause me to prefer some of their works over others. Yet the fact that they have been able to sustain the energy to survive for decades as professional novelists, garnering a solid group of readers along the way, tells me that they must somehow be endowed with a core of steel. An intrinsic, internal drive compelling them to write. A tenacious, persevering temperament that equips them to work long and lonely hours. It is my belief that these are the qualifications required of a professional novelist.

It's not difficult to write a single novel. Even a very good novel, depending on who you are. It isn't easy to pull off, but it's not impossible. What's really hard is to keep on writing novels year after year. That's not something just anyone can do. As I have pointed out, it requires a special set of qualifications. Qualifications that may be based on something quite different than "talent."

So how do you discover if you have what it takes to be a novelist? There is only one answer: you have to jump in the water and see if you sink or swim. I know this sounds blunt, but when you get right down to it, I guess that's the way life is. You can live wisely and well without writing a novel—in fact, it may be easier that way. Those who end up writing a novel do so because they have to. And then they continue. As a fellow novelist, I embrace them with open arms.

Welcome to the ring!

When I Became a Novelist

↳

WHEN I MADE my literary debut by winning the Gunzo Prize for New Writers, I was thirty years old, with a fair amount of life experience under my belt. The nature of that experience, however, diverged somewhat from the norm. In those days, most guys graduated from college, found work, and then, when things leveled off, got married. That's what I expected to do as well. Or at least that's what I figured would happen. It was the way of the world, after all. I had no intention to contravene (for better or for worse) what seemed to be the dictates of common sense. Yet as things turned out, I got married first, found work, and then, after some time passed, finally got around to completing my degree. In other words, I followed the exact opposite of the prescribed order. It was just the way things happened—our futures, it seems, don't always unfold in the ways that we expect.

At any rate, having started out by getting married (it's a very long story, so I won't go into details), and hating the prospect of working for a company (those reasons would also take a long time to explain, so I'll omit them, too), I decided that I wanted to open a jazz café, a place that served coffee, drinks, and some food. I was totally absorbed by jazz back then (I still listen to it quite a bit), so I was drawn to the idea of listening to the music I loved from morning to night. Marrying while still in school, however, meant that we had no money. So for the next three years, my wife and I took whatever work we could find to raise enough capital. We also borrowed money from everyone we could think of. In the end, we had a sufficient amount to open a café near the south exit of Kokubunji Station in western Tokyo. The year was 1974.

Fortunately for us, it was a time when, unlike today, young people could still start small businesses without a huge pile of money. Many of us detested corporations and the idea of selling out to "the system," which meant that enterprises like ours were opening right and left: coffee shops, restaurants, variety stores, bookstores. A number were close by, all run by people about our age. There were also young radicals, wannabe members of the student movement, hanging around the neighborhood. All over the world, you could still find small niches in which to live. If you could locate one you could fit into, you could get by somehow. Things could get wild at times, but it was an interesting era.

I brought my old piano from home, and we began to feature live music on weekends. Many jazz musicians lived in the Musashino area, where Kokubunji is located, and everyone was happy (I think) to play for the pittance I could offer. The list included Shigeharu Mukai, Aki Takase, Kiyoshi Sugimoto, Yoshio Otomo, Takao Uematsu, Ryojiro Furusawa, and Fumio Watanabe. We were all young then, full of ambition and energy—though, sad to say, no one was making any money to speak of.

I loved what I was doing, but we had borrowed an awful lot of money and had to sweat to pay it back. Some of our debt was owed to the bank, and some to our friends. We paid the friends back in just a few years, with interest—what else could we do? But to do that, we had to work from morning until night and skimp on food. We ("we" being my wife and myself) lived a very frugal, Spartan life in those days. We had no TV or radio—not even an alarm clock. Nor was there any real way to heat our room, so when the nights were cold, we slept huddled together, clinging to our cats. The cats clung desperately to us as well.

One night my wife and I were trudging home with our heads down, too broke to make the bank payment that was due the next day, when we stumbled upon a crumpled wad of bills lying in the street. Whether it was synchronicity or some kind of sign, I don't know, but strange to say, it was exactly the amount we needed. It really saved us, since otherwise our check would have bounced. (For some reason, strange things like this happen from time to time in my life.) We should have turned the money in to the police, but we were strapped, so we kept it. There isn't much point in apologizing now. I guess I'll have to repay my debt to society through other means.

I don't mean to go on and on about how hard we had it, only to stress that life wasn't easy when I was in my twenties. Certainly there were others who were far worse off than me. From their vantage point, the way I lived would hardly qualify as "rough." I can't disagree with that; yet even so, it was plenty harsh enough for me. That's all I want to say.

Still, it was fun. No doubt there. I was young and strong, and able to listen to the music that I loved all day as the ruler of my own little domain. I didn't have to commute to work on packed rush-hour trains or attend boring meetings or suck up to a boss I disliked. And I was blessed with the chance to meet some really fascinating people.

I learned a lot about the world during those years too. "Learning about the world" sounds rather presumptuous, but what I mean is that I grew up. It was a perilous time, spent banging my head against the wall and fighting my way through. Terrible things were said and done to me, things that often left me frustrated and bitter. In those days, working in the entertainment industry—the "water trade," as it's called in Japan—meant putting up with a good deal of social prejudice. I worked myself to the bone and held my tongue about lots of things. I had to learn how to toss angry drunks out of the café and how to keep my head down when an ill wind blew. All I had time to think about was paying back what we owed and keeping the business afloat.

This desperate frame of mind helped get me through the hard years without major injury until, somehow, I came out on the other side into a space that was slightly more open and relaxed. When I stopped to rest and looked around, I discovered—to put it as plainly as I can—a landscape I had never seen before stretching before my eyes, and a new me standing there looking at it. I was slightly tougher than before, I realized, and a (very little) bit wiser.

Now I am not suggesting that the more hardship you endure the better off you will be. If you manage to get through this life without suffering, so much the better. I know there is nothing at all pleasant about hardship—it can drive you so low you can't get up again. Nevertheless, if you are dealing with adverse conditions and the painful thoughts that come in their wake, you should take it from me that what you're going through now may bear fruit down the road. I don't know if this will help or not, but you should try to bear it in mind and keep moving forward.

Looking back, I think I was just an "average boy" until I started working. I grew up in a quiet suburb in the Kobe and Osaka district without either causing or experiencing any special problems, and managed to do so-so in school without working very hard. One thing I always loved, though, was reading. I doubt any of my peers in junior high and high school read as many books as I did. I was also absorbed in listening to all kinds of music. As a result, I spent little time studying. I was an only child, well looked after (in other words, spoiled), who had led a protected life. In short, I was hopelessly ignorant of the world.

I entered Waseda University in Tokyo in the late 1960s at the peak of the student protests; the university was shut down and the gates closed for long stretches while I was there. At first, the cause was a massive student strike; later, it was the university that locked us out. Almost all classes were suspended during this time, which meant that (luckily?) my college days were a pretty haphazard affair.

I have never been comfortable in groups or in any kind of collective action with others, so I didn't become a member of any student groups, but I did support the movement in a general sort of way and tried to do what I could within my own private circle. As time passed, however, and internecine warfare between the student factions grew more and more violent and senseless—an apolitical student was murdered in the classroom we often used, for example—many of us became disenchanted. Something criminally wrong had wormed its way into the movement. The positive power of imagination had been lost. I felt this strongly. As a result, when the storm passed, all we were left with was the bitter taste of disappointment. Uplifting slogans and beautiful messages might stir the soul, but if they weren't accompanied by moral power they amounted to no more than a litany of empty words. That was the lesson I took away from those events, a lesson that has only been confirmed by everything I have seen since. Words have power. Yet that power must be rooted in truth and justice. Words must never stand apart from those principles.

From that point on, I shifted my focus once again, this time to more private things—namely, the world of books, music, and movies. For a considerable time I worked at night in the Kabukicho area of downtown Tokyo, where I encountered a wide variety of people. I don't know what Kabukicho is like these days, but back then it was a fascinating place, with sketchy characters of all kinds clustered on every corner. These were interesting and fun times, but things could also get intense and even a little dangerous. Whatever the case, though, I'm pretty sure I learned more about life in its many forms and grew appreciably wiser hanging around such a lively place with its motley—albeit rough and occasionally unsavory—crowd than I would have in a college classroom, or with a group of people much like myself. In short, I became streetwise. That gritty environment was a much better fit for me than university life would have been. I just couldn't get into studying.

As I was already married and working, I had passed the point when a college degree would have been helpful. Nevertheless, since the Waseda University system at the time allowed credits to be purchased on a course-by-course basis, and I had accumulated almost enough to graduate, I managed to find time outside work to attend classes and finish within seven years of when I started. In my final year, I enrolled in a course on Racine taught by Professor Shinya Ando, but my spotty attendance meant I was bound to fail, so I went to his office. "With a wife and a full-time job, I have a hard time getting to class," I explained, whereupon he came all the way out to my club in Kokubunji to see for himself. "Yeah, you've got it pretty rough," he said, and gave me the credit I needed to graduate. I don't know how things are today, but back then there were quite a few bighearted professors like that. Can't remember much about his lectures, though (sorry!).

For three years, I ran my jazz café in the basement of the building near Kokubunji Station's south exit. We attracted enough customers to start paying back our debts, but then, quite suddenly, the owner ordered us out, saying that he wanted to make the building bigger. Resigning ourselves (he really screwed us over, but if I get into that there'll be no end), we looked around and found a place in Sendagaya in downtown Tokyo. It was brighter than our Kokubunji digs and big enough to install a grand piano for live performances, but that also meant that we had to borrow more money, so we couldn't take it easy. (Not being able to "take it easy" seems to form the leitmotif of my life!)

It was thus that I spent my twenties laboring from morning to night to pay off debts. All I can remember of that decade, in fact, is how hard I worked. I imagine others have a lot more fun in their twenties, but I had neither the time nor the money to enjoy the "sweet days of youth." Still, I read whenever I had the chance. Life might have been hectic and things might have been rough, but the joy I took in books and music never wavered. That, at least, was something no one could take from me.

As the end of my twenties approached, our Sendagaya jazz café was, at last, beginning to show signs of stability. True, we couldn't sit back and relax—we still owed money, and our business had its ups and downs—but at least things seemed to be headed in a good direction.

I have no special talent for business, nor am I particularly friendly or social, which makes me ill suited to deal with customers. Yet I do have one redeeming feature—I work my butt off when I'm engaged in something I like. This, I think, is why our café did pretty well. Jazz was one of my great loves, after all, so I was basically quite happy with my work. One day, however, it hit me that I was pushing thirty. What I thought of as my youth was coming to a close. I remember how weird that feeling was. "So this is how it is," I thought. "Time just slips away."

ONE BRIGHT April afternoon in 1978, I attended a baseball game at Jingu Stadium in downtown Tokyo. It was the Central League season opener, first pitch at one o'clock, the Yakult Swallows against the Hiroshima Carp. I was already a Yakult fan in those days, and the stadium was close to my apartment (not far from Sendagaya's Hatonomori Hachiman Shrine), so I sometimes popped in to catch a game when I was out for a stroll.

Back then, Yakult was a perennially weak team, with little money and no flashy big-name players. Naturally, they weren't very popular. Season opener it may have been, but only a few fans were sitting beyond the outfield fence. I stretched out with a beer to watch the game. At the time there were no bleacher seats, just a grassy slope. It was a great feeling. The sky was a sparkling blue, the draft beer as cold as cold could be, and the ball strikingly white against the green field, the first green I had seen in a long time. To fully appreciate a baseball game, you really have to be there in person!

Yakult's first batter was Dave Hilton, a rangy newcomer from the United States and a complete unknown. He batted in the lead-off position. The cleanup hitter was Charlie Manuel, who later became famous as the manager of the Philadelphia Phillies. Then, though, he was a real stud, a slugger Japanese fans had dubbed "the Red Demon."

I think Hiroshima's starting pitcher that day was Satoshi Taka-hashi. Yakult countered with Takeshi Yasuda. In the bottom of the first inning, Hilton slammed Takahashi's first pitch into left field for a clean double. The satisfying crack when bat met ball resounded through Jingu Stadium. Scattered applause rose around me. In that instant, and based on no grounds whatsoever, it suddenly struck me: *I think I can write a novel.*

I can still recall the exact sensation. It was as if something had come fluttering down from the sky and I had caught it cleanly in my hands. I had no idea why it had *chanced* to fall into my grasp. I didn't know then, and I don't know now. Whatever the reason, *it* had taken place. It was like a revelation. Or maybe "epiphany" is a better word. All I can say is that my life was drastically and perma-nently altered in that instant when leadoff batter Dave Hilton belted that beautiful ringing double at Jingu Stadium.

After the game (Yakult won, as I recall), I took the train to Shin-juku, went to the Kinokuniya bookstore, picked up a sheaf of writ-ing paper, and splurged on a Sailor fountain pen for two thousand yen. Word processors and computers weren't around back then, which meant I had to write everything by hand, one character at a time. The sensation of writing felt very fresh. I was thrilled. It had been such a long time since I had put fountain pen to paper.

Each night after that, when I got home from work, I sat at my kitchen table and wrote. Those few hours before dawn were practi-cally the only time I had free. Over the six or so months that fol-lowed, I wrote *Hear the Wind Sing* (though it had another title at that stage). I wrapped up the first draft right when baseball season ended. Incidentally, that year the Yakult Swallows bucked the odds and almost everyone's predictions to win the Central League pennant, then went on to defeat the Pacific League champions—the pitching-rich Hankyu Braves—in the Japan Series. It was a glorious, miraculous season.

HEAR THE WIND SING is a short novel, less than two hundred manuscript pages long. Yet it took many months and much effort to complete. Part of the reason, of course, was the limited time I had to work on it, but the real problem was that I hadn't a clue how to write a novel. To tell the truth, although I had been absorbed in reading all kinds of stuff—my favorites being translations of Russian novels and English-language paperbacks—I had never read modern Japanese novels (of the "serious" variety) in any concerted way. Thus I had no idea what kind of Japanese literature was being read at the time or how I should write fiction in the Japanese language.

For several months, I operated on pure guesswork, adopting what seemed to be a likely style and running with it, but when I read through the result I was far from impressed. "Good grief," I moaned, "this is hopeless." What I had written seemed to fulfill the formal requirements of a novel, yet it was rather boring and, as a whole, left me cold. "If that's the way the author feels," I thought dejectedly, "a reader will react even more negatively. Looks like I just don't have what it takes." Under normal circumstances, it would have ended there—I would have walked away. But the epiphany I had received on Jingu Stadium's grassy slope was still clearly etched in my mind.

In retrospect, it was only natural that I was unable to produce a good novel. It was a big mistake to assume that a guy like me who had never written anything in his life could spin out something brilliant right off the bat. Maybe it had been a mistake to try to write something "novelistic" in the first place. "Give up trying to create something sophisticated," I told myself. "Why not forget all those prescriptive ideas about 'the novel' and 'literature' and set down your feelings and thoughts as they come to you, freely, in a way that you like?"

While it was easy to talk about setting down one's impressions freely, though, actually doing it wasn't that simple. For a sheer beginner like myself, it was virtually impossible. To make a fresh start, the first thing I had to do was ditch my stack of manuscript paper and my fountain pen. As long as they were sitting in front of me, what I was doing felt like "literature." In their place, I pulled out my old Olivetti typewriter from the closet. Then, as an experiment, I decided to write the opening of my novel in English. What the hell, I figured. If I was going to do something unorthodox, why not go all the way?

Needless to say, my ability in English composition didn't amount to much. My vocabulary was severely limited, as was my command of English syntax. I could only write in short, simple sentences. Which meant that, however complex and numerous the thoughts running around in my head, I couldn't even attempt to set them down as they came to me. The language had to be simple, my ideas expressed in an easy-to-understand way, the descriptions stripped of all extraneous fat, the form made compact, and everything arranged to fit a container of limited size. The result was a rough, uncultivated kind of prose. As I struggled to express myself in that fashion, however, a distinctive rhythm began to take shape.

I was born and raised in Japan, so the vocabulary and patterns of Japanese—in short, the language's contents—had filled the system that was *me* to bursting. When I sought to put my thoughts and feelings into words, those contents began to swirl like mad, and the system sometimes crashed. Writing in a foreign language, with all the limitations that it entailed, removed this obstacle. It also led me to the realization that I could express my thoughts and feelings with a limited set of words and grammatical structures, as long as I combined them effectively and linked them together in a skillful manner. Ultimately, I learned that there was no need for a lot of difficult words—I didn't have to try to impress people with beautiful turns of phrase.

Much later, I found out that the writer Ágota Kristóf had written a number of wonderful novels in a style that had a very similar effect. Kristóf was a Hungarian citizen who left Hungary in 1956 during the upheaval there for Switzerland, where she began to write in French. She did so partly out of necessity, since there was no way she could make a living writing novels in Hungarian. Yet it was through writing in a foreign language that she succeeded in developing a style that was new and uniquely hers. It featured a strong rhythm based on short sentences, diction that was never roundabout but always straightforward, and description that was to the point and free of emotional baggage. Her novels were cloaked in an air of mystery hinting at important matters hidden beneath the surface. Later, when I first encountered her work, it made me feel quite nostalgic, although her literary inclinations are obviously different than mine.

Having discovered the curious effect of composing in a foreign language, thereby acquiring a creative rhythm distinctly my own, I returned my Olivetti to the closet and once more pulled out my sheaf of manuscript paper and my fountain pen. Then I sat down and "translated" the chapter or so that I had written in English into Japanese. Well, "transplanted" might be more accurate, since it wasn't a direct verbatim translation. In the process, inevitably, a new style of Japanese emerged. The style that became mine, one that I had discovered. "Now I get it," I thought. "This is how I should be doing it." It was a moment of true clarity, when the scales fell from my eyes.

Some people have said, "Your work has the feel of translation." The precise meaning of this statement escapes me, but I think it may hit the mark in one way and entirely miss it in another. Since the opening passages of my first novella were, quite literally, "translated," the comment is not entirely wrong; yet it applies merely to my process of writing. What I was seeking by writing first in English and then "translating" into Japanese was no less than the creation of an unadorned "neutral" style that would allow me freer movement. My interest was not in creating a watered-down form of Japanese. Rather, I wanted to deploy a type of Japanese as far removed as possible from the strictures of "serious literature" in order to speak in my own natural voice. That required desperate measures. I would go so far as to say that, at that time, I may have regarded Japanese as no more than a functional tool.

Some see this as an affront to our national language. In fact, I have been criticized on precisely those grounds. Language, though, is tough and resilient, a tenacity backed up by a long history. Its autonomy cannot be lost or seriously damaged, however roughly it is handled. It is the right of all writers to experiment with the possibilities of language and expand the range of its effectiveness. Without that adventurous spirit, nothing new can ever be born. In a certain way, I continue to regard Japanese as a kind of tool, even today. I would even say that explorations into its "toolness" may lead to the regeneration of the Japanese language.

At any rate, I rewrote the "rather boring" novel I had just finished from top to bottom in the new style that I had just developed. Although the story line remained more or less intact, the mode of expression was entirely different. Different, too, was its impact on the reader. It was, of course, the short novel *Hear the Wind Sing*. I wasn't entirely satisfied with the way it turned out. When I reread it, I found it immature and riddled with faults. Only twenty to thirty percent of what I was trying to say came across. Yet it was my first novel, and I had managed to write in a form that somehow worked, so I was left with the feeling that I had taken a big first step. To put it another way, I felt as though I had realized some of the promise carried to me by my "epiphany."

Writing in my new style felt more like performing music than composing literature, a feeling that stays with me today. It was as if the words were coming through my body instead of from my head. Sustaining the rhythm, finding the coolest chords, trusting in the power of improvisation—it was tremendously exciting. When I sat down at the kitchen table each night and went back to work on my novel (if that's what it was) using my new style, I felt like I was holding a new, cutting-edge tool in my hands. Boy oh boy, was it fun! And it filled the spiritual void that had loomed with the approach of my thirtieth birthday.

This radical shift would be more apparent if I could compare *Hear the Wind Sing* with its "rather boring" predecessor, but, unfortunately, I threw the latter away. Nor do I have any clear memory of what it was like. I know now that I should have held on to it, but it was useless as far as I could see, so I threw it in the trash without a second thought. Now all I can recall is that it wasn't much fun to write. Hardly surprising, given the sort of style I was using. The problem was that it had not flowed naturally. Writing in that style had been like exercising in clothes that didn't fit.

IT WAS A SUNNY Sunday morning in spring when I got the call from an editor at the literary journal *Gunzo* telling me that *Hear the Wind Sing* had been short-listed for their Prize for New Writers. Almost a year had passed since the season opener at Jingu Stadium, and I had already turned thirty. It was around eleven a.m., but I was still fast asleep, having worked very late the night before. I picked up the receiver, but I was so groggy I had no idea at first who was on the other end or what he was trying to say. To tell the truth, by that time I had quite forgotten having sent *Hear the Wind Sing* to *Gunzo*. Once I had finished the manuscript and put it in someone else's hands, my desire to write had completely subsided. Composing it had been, so to speak, an act of defiance— I had written it very easily, just as it came to me—so the idea that it might make the short list had never occurred to me. In fact, I had sent them my only copy. If they hadn't selected it, it probably would have vanished forever. I probably never would have written another novel. Life is strange, when you think about it.

The editor told me there were five finalists, including me. I was surprised. But I was also very sleepy, so the reality of what had happened didn't really sink in. I got out of bed, washed, dressed, and went out for a walk with my wife. Just when we were passing Sendagaya Elementary School on Meiji Avenue, I noticed a carrier pigeon hiding in the shrubbery. I saw that it seemed to have a broken wing, so I picked it up. A metal tag was affixed to its leg. Cradling it in my hands, I carried it to the small police station in Omotesando, adjacent to the Dojunkai-Aoyama Apartments (the present home of Omotesando Hills). As I walked along the side streets of Harajuku, the warmth of the wounded pigeon sank into my hands. I felt it quivering. That Sunday was bright and clear, and the trees, the buildings, and the shop windows sparkled in the spring sunlight.

That's when it hit me. I was going to win the prize. And I was going to go on to become a novelist who would enjoy some degree of success. It was an audacious presumption, but for some reason I was sure at that moment that it would happen. Completely sure. Not in a theoretical way, but directly and intuitively.

I CAN STILL REMEMBER, with total clarity, how I felt when whatever it was came fluttering down into my hands that day thirty years ago on the grass behind the outfield fence at Jingu Stadium; and I recall just as clearly the warmth of the wounded pigeon in those same hands that spring afternoon a year later, near Sendagaya Elementary School. I always call up those sensations when I think about what it means to write a novel. Such tactile memories have taught me to trust in that *something* I carry within me and to dream of the possibilities it offers. How wonderful it is that these sensations still reside within me!

THERE IS NO basic change today—I feel the same pleasure and excitement I felt when I wrote my first novel. I wake up early, brew fresh coffee in the kitchen, pour some in a big mug, sit down at my desk, and boot up my computer (there are times, I must admit, when I miss the days of manuscript sheets and my fat Montblanc fountain pen). Then I sit there and muse about what to write that day. Such moments are pure bliss. To tell the truth, I have never found writing painful. Neither (thankfully) have I ever found myself unable to write. What's the point of writing, anyway, if you're not enjoying it? I can't get my head around the idea of "the suffering writer." Basically, I think, novels should emerge in a spontaneous flow.

I do not consider myself a genius in any way, shape, or form. Nor do I think I am equipped with some special sort of talent. Of course, the fact that I have been able to make a living as a professional writer for over thirty years means that I am not entirely lacking in ability. I guess something within me—some aspect of my temperament, perhaps—must have been at work from the beginning. That line of thinking, though, has no payoff for me. I'll leave it for someone else—if, in fact, such a person exists—to carry forward.

What has been (and continues to be) most important for me is my direct, physical awareness that some special power has *given me the chance* to write novels. I have been able to grasp that opportunity and, with no little help from Lady Luck, turn it into a career. Looking back, I have no idea who granted me this license, only that someone or something did. All I can say is that I am truly grateful. And that I will treasure it—as I treasured that wounded pigeon—while I go on happily turning out my fiction. What comes after that is anybody's guess.

On Literary Prizes

N E X T , I think I'd like to move on to talk about literary prizes. Let's start with a concrete example, the Ryūnosuke Akutagawa Prize. This is a sensitive, rather tricky topic for me, which makes it somewhat awkward, but I think it's a story I should tell at this juncture, even at the risk of being misunderstood. That's the feeling I have, anyway. Moreover, talking about the Akutagawa Prize is a good introduction to talking about prizes more generally, while talking about prizes may be a good angle from which to approach one aspect of the literary world in modern Japan.

I WAS LEAFING THROUGH a literary journal not long ago when I came across a column at the back that included the following passage: "What a magical allure the Akutagawa Prize possesses! The commotion stirred up by the writers who don't win serves merely to enhance its reputation, while its growing authority is confirmed by the case of Haruki Murakami, who removed himself from the literary world after being dropped from the running." The author's name was listed as Yuyu Aima, clearly a pseudonym.

It is a fact that over thirty years ago, two of my works were shortlisted for the Akutagawa Prize and both failed to win. Since then, I have pursued my work quite removed from what might be called the literary world. These two facts, however, are unrelated: that I didn't (or couldn't) win bears no connection whatsoever to my distance from the literary world, a place I knew little about and had no desire to set foot in. It annoys me that someone has, quite arbitrarily, tried to create a cause-and-effect relationship between the two.

There may be readers who believed this story. In a worst-case scenario, it might even become the standard version. I have always thought that writing was based on the ability to distinguish between inference and assertion, but I guess that isn't the case. Perhaps I should be happy that the word on the street today is that I "removed myself," unlike in the old days, when I was supposedly "rejected" by the literary establishment.

ONE FACTOR that helps explain my relative distance from the literary world is that I never set out to become a writer in the first place. I was just a regular guy who in his spare time tossed off a novel that happened to go on to win a new writers' prize. As a result, I knew very little about the literary world and the awards they hand out.

I also had a full-time job, which meant that my hands were full taking care of the many things I had to look after. I was too busy, in fact, to think of anything other than what was absolutely necessary (a few clones would have been useful!). Once I had become a full-time writer, I was less busy, but because of my conscious decision, my schedule involved waking up and going to bed early, as well as regular physical workouts, so that I seldom went out at night. Not once, for example, did I visit those writers' watering holes clustered in the Golden Street area not far from Shinjuku Station, where so much literary socializing takes place. It's not that I felt any antipathy toward Golden Street and its inhabitants. Rather, I lacked the time or the need to go there—in practical terms, there was just no reason to go.

I have no idea whether or not the Akutagawa Prize possesses any "magical allure" or "authority." I have never given the matter any thought. If there is a magical allure of the sort the author of the column describes, it certainly hasn't found its way to my neck of the woods. Perhaps it took the wrong road.

Although my first two novels, *Hear the Wind Sing* and *Pinball, 1973*, were short-listed for the Akutagawa Prize, to tell the truth (and I hope you believe me when I say this) I really didn't care if they won or lost.

I had been overjoyed, however, when *Hear the Wind Sing* had won the Gunzo Prize. I don't mind telling that to the world. It was truly a landmark event in my life, my ticket to becoming a writer. With it, I was guaranteed entry; without it, the story might have ended very differently. Doors began to open to me. With that ticket in hand, I thought, anything was possible. I had no time to spare to think one way or the other about the Akutagawa Prize.

Another thing was that I really didn't consider my first two novels all that good. I knew in my heart that they only represented a small fraction—maybe twenty or thirty percent—of what I was capable of doing. I had never written anything before and had mastered none of the basic skills needed to put together a novel. Looking back, I think that it's *possible* that the two books are actually *better* precisely because I was working at only twenty or thirty percent of my full capacity. At any rate, I was dissatisfied with a lot of things in those first two works.

Therefore, while receiving the Prize for New Writers was a great help, winning the Akutagawa Prize at that juncture might have been a hindrance, a burden of high expectations I would have had to carry forward. At my stage of development, it seemed a bit too much.

Give me time, I thought, and I can turn out something much better. This may sound arrogant for someone who not long before had never given a thought to writing a novel. It even sounds arrogant to me. In all honesty, though, anyone who lacks that level of arrogance is unlikely to become a novelist.

THE MEDIA HAD LISTED both *Hear the Wind Sing* and *Pinball, 1973* as favorites to win the Akutagawa Prize, but although those around me were disappointed, I myself was relieved not to have won, for the reasons I have previously mentioned. I could also understand how the jury members felt rejecting my work. "I guess that's the way things are" was more or less my attitude. At least I didn't bear any grudges. Nor did I try to stack up what I had done against the other works under consideration.

My relief also stemmed from the fact that I would not have to deal with the publicity that would follow winning the Akutagawa Prize, which would have disrupted my daily life. I had no choice but to hobnob with the people who came to the jazz café. In that line of work, you're not supposed to simply disappear when patrons appear whom you don't want to meet (although there were times I got so fed up I did just that).

After I had been passed over twice for the Akutagawa Prize, I was informed by my editors that I was now considered "used goods," and should not expect to be nominated again. I remember how weird that felt. Since the Akutagawa is meant for new writers, unsuccessful candidates are dropped from their list at a certain point. Although the columnist who described this situation reported that some writers were considered as many as six times, I was "used goods" after only two kicks at the can. I don't know how or why that came about, but whatever the circumstances, apparently the fact that Haruki Murakami was "used goods" quickly became the consensus throughout the literary establishment. That's how they operate, I guess.

Still, I wasn't overly disappointed to have become "used goods." In fact, it was a relief not to have to think further about the Akutagawa Prize. I remember how strangely antsy the people around me got as decision day approached—that bothered me more than whether I won or not. I could feel their expectations mounting, and with them something like a mild irritation. My candidacy was also picked up by the media, which elicited a bigger response, and some backlash, adding to my woes. Given that these two occasions led to such gloomy repercussions, it was depressing to think it might continue year after year.

What weighed on me the most were the reactions of those who tried to console me. No sooner had the results been announced than a stream of people would show up to give me a pep talk. "Too bad this time," they would say. "But don't worry—you'll win it next time around." I knew that by and large, they were saying this out of kindness, but all the same I had a hard time finding the right words to respond. I mean, I had to say something—I couldn't just go through the motions. If I had confessed that I really didn't care that much, though, they would have refused to take what I said at face value, and both of us would have been made uncomfortable.

NHK created problems, too. No sooner was my candidacy announced than they phoned asking me to go on TV if I won. Given my busy schedule and the fact that I hated appearing in public (it's just not my thing), I refused, but instead of backing off they became more insistent, sometimes even angry. In short, candidacy for the Akutagawa Prize brought me nothing but headaches.

WHY DOES THE PUBLIC get so wrapped up in the Akutagawa Prize? It sometimes baffles me. Not long ago, for example, I was visiting a bookstore when I saw a stack of a book titled *The Reasons Haruki Murakami Failed to Win the Akutagawa Prize* or something like that. I haven't read it—how could I buy something with such an embarrassing title?—so I don't know what those "reasons" are, but I can't help finding it strange that such a book would be published in the first place.

If I had won the Akutagawa Prize, what possible difference would it have made to my life or to the fate of the world at large? The world would be more or less as it is today, while my writing would have proceeded at about the same pace, give or take a few minor differences along the way, for the past thirty-odd years. With or without the prize, my novels would have been embraced by the same readers, and would have ticked off the same people as well (I seem to have a talent for rubbing people the wrong way).

If winning the Akutagawa Prize meant that the war in Iraq might not have happened or something of that sort, I'm sure I would feel terrible. Since that's not the case, however, why on earth would anyone bother to write a book on the topic? I just can't get my head around it. This "controversy" is too trivial to be called a tempest in a teapot—it's more like a tiny dust devil.

At the risk of causing offense, I should state the obvious: the Akutagawa Prize is just another literary award presided over by the Bungei Shunju publishing house. Its purpose may not be strictly commercial, but it would be folly to pretend that Bungei Shunju's bottom line is not involved.

Be that as it may, as someone who has been a novelist for a long time, it is my experience that a new writer whose work deserves close attention comes along only once every five years or so. Maybe once every three years, if we relax our standards. The Akutagawa Prize, on the other hand, is handed out twice a year, which means its quality tends to be watered down. Though I have no argument with that (prizes can be seen as congratulatory gifts aimed at encouraging new writers, providing a entry point for more rookies), it does make me wonder about the circus atmosphere the media creates each time around. Looked at objectively, it all seems out of proportion.

If we expand the discussion to include not just the Akutagawa Prize but the value of literary prizes everywhere, then we run up against a wall. That's because there is no basis, again objectively speaking, for the true value of any prize, from the Oscars to the Nobel, except of course in those special cases where the criteria are based on a numerical assessment. If you start picking holes in how they make their decisions, there is no end to it. If you worship the award, however, there is no end to that, either.

This is what Raymond Chandler said about the Nobel Prize in one of his letters: "Do I wish to be a great writer?" he wrote. "Do I wish to win the Nobel Prize? Not if it takes much hard work. What the hell, they give the Nobel Prize to too many second-raters for me to get excited about it. Besides, I'd have to go to Sweden and dress up and make a speech. Is the Nobel Prize worth all that? Hell, no."[1]

American novelist Nelson Algren (*The Man with the Golden Arm, A Walk on the Wild Side*) won the National Institute of Arts and Letters Award of Merit Medal in 1974 thanks to the support of Kurt Vonnegut, but he blew off the awards ceremony and got drunk with a woman at a bar instead. Of course, his absence was intentional. When asked "What'd you do with the medal?" Algren answered: "I dunno, I threw it away or something."[2]

These two writers may have been extreme exceptions. They wrote in unique styles and stood against the establishment throughout their lives. Yet the feeling they shared, or perhaps what they wished to express through their attitudes, was that there are more important things to a true writer than literary prizes. One of those things was the conviction that what they wrote had real meaning; another was that they were speaking to a community of readers—the number wasn't really that important—who understood what that meaning was. Writers convinced of those two things have little use for prizes and awards. In the end, after all, honors are merely a formal social and literary ratification of an existing reality.

Still, many in the world pay attention solely to things that possess visible and concrete *form*. Literary quality is inherently formless, so prizes, medals, and such provide that concreteness. This "form" then induces people to look. What really rubbed Chandler and Algren the wrong way was the decidedly nonliterary quality of the awards and the overbearing arrogance exhibited by the authorities, whose attitude was "The prize is yours only if you come to receive it."

I have a standard answer when interviewers ask me about literary prizes—this question invariably comes up, whether in Japan or abroad. "The most important thing," I tell them, "is good readers. Nothing means as much as the people who dip into their pockets to buy my books—not prizes, or medals, or critical praise." I repeat this answer over and over ad nauseam, yet it doesn't seem to sink in. Most often it's completely ignored.

When I stop to think about it, though, interviewers may simply find my answer boring. There may be something about it that sounds packaged for public consumption. I sometimes get that feeling, too. It certainly isn't the kind of comment that sparks a journalist's interest. Nevertheless, since the answer reflects what I see as the honest truth, I can't really change it, however boring it may be. That's why I end up saying the same thing time and again. Readers have no ulterior motives when they shell out twenty or thirty dollars for one of my books. "Let's check this out" is (probably) what they're thinking, pure and simple. Or they may be full of anticipation. I am eternally grateful to such readers. Compared to them . . . no, let's just drop the comparisons.

At the risk of stating the obvious, it is literary works that last, not literary prizes. I doubt many can tell you who won the Akutagawa Prize two years ago, or the Nobel Prize winner three years back. Can you? Truly great works that have stood the test of time, on the other hand, are lodged in our memory forever. Was Ernest Hemingway a Nobel Prize winner? (He was.) How about Jorge Luis Borges? (Was he? Who gives a damn?) A literary prize can turn the spotlight on a particular work, but it can't breathe life into it. It's that simple.

WHAT HAS NOT WINNING the Akutagawa cost me? I have turned the question over in my mind, but can't come up with anything. Have I gained something? No, that's not true, either.

Still, perhaps I am fortunate not to have the title "Akutagawa Prize Winner" affixed to my name. Otherwise (and this is pure conjecture on my part), it might be suggested that it was somehow thanks to the prize that I have reached this point, which I would probably find upsetting. Life is more free and easy without such titles. Being only Haruki Murakami is just fine with me. And if I'm not bothered, what's the big fuss?

I bear no animosity whatsoever toward the Akutagawa Prize (I feel the need to keep emphasizing this), but I must admit that I am proud to have written my novels and lived my life as an independent agent. It may be a trivial thing, but for me at least it carries some weight.

It's a very rough estimate, but my guess is that about five percent of all people are active readers of literature. This narrow slice of the population forms the core of the total reading public. There is a lot of talk today about people becoming estranged from books and the written word, and I must admit I see that, too, but I imagine that five percent would find a way to read somehow or other even if the authorities ordered them to stop. They might not take refuge in the forest and commit books to memory as in Ray Bradbury's *Fahrenheit 451*, but I'm sure they would escape the crackdown and keep on reading somehow. Of course I would be among them.

Once the habit of reading has taken hold—usually when we are very young—it cannot be easily dislodged. YouTube and 3D videos may be within easy reach, but when we five-percenters have free time (and even when we don't), we reach for a book. As long as one in twenty is like us, I refuse to get overly worried about the future of the novel and the written word. Nor do I see the electronic media as a threat. The form and the medium aren't all that important, and I don't care if the words appear on paper or on a screen (or are transmitted orally, à la *Fahrenheit 451*). As long as book lovers keep on reading books, I'm happy.

My only serious concern is this: *What can I offer those book lovers next?* All other questions are peripheral. After all, five percent of the Japanese population adds up to six million people. Shouldn't a writer be able to keep his or her head above water with a market of that size? If you look beyond Japan to the rest of the world, the number of readers increases that much more.

But what about the other ninety-five percent? They have few opportunities to encounter literature face-to-face in their daily lives, and those chances may grow even slimmer in the future. The move away from reading may continue. Yet, from what I can see, at least half of those people—another very rough estimate—might take a work of literature in hand and read it if they had the chance, either as a sociocultural phenomenon or as intellectual entertainment. These are the latent readers, the "undecided voters" in political terms. They need a welcome counter to usher them into the world of literature. Or maybe something like a showroom. Perhaps this is (and has been) the job of the Akutagawa Prize, to act as a welcome counter for new readers. It could be compared to Beaujolais Nouveau or the Vienna New Year's Concert or the Hakone Ekiden relay; in short, to those entry points into the worlds of wine, classical music, and marathon running. Then, of course, there is the Nobel Prize for Literature. It is when we come to the case of the Nobel, though, that things become more complicated.

I have never served on a selection jury for any literary prize. I have been asked, but have always politely refused. That is because I feel I am not qualified for the task.

The reason is a simple one—I am just too much of an individualist. I am a person with a fixed vision and a fixed process for giving that vision shape. Unavoidably, sustaining that process entails an all-encompassing lifestyle. Without that, I cannot write.

That is my yardstick, my recipe for success, but although it works for me, I doubt it would be suitable for other writers. I cannot pretend that my way is the only way, and I respect many of the other methods adopted by writers all over the world—yet there are approaches that I find incompatible or that I just can't get my head around. I am the sort of person who can only appraise things that fit with his own viewpoint. Looked at positively, this is an example of individualism; negatively, the mark of a self-centered and egotistic person. Were I to extend this self-centered focus and use it as a yardstick to evaluate the works of other writers, they would likely find it intolerable. Experienced writers might be able to handle it, but I shudder to think how those just starting out might react to having their fates influenced by a viewpoint as slanted as mine. I just can't do it.

Should someone attack me for having abandoned my social responsibility as a writer, I would have to confess he or she might have a point. After all, it was thanks to the Gunzo Prize for New Writers that I got my start—it was at their gate, so to speak, that I got my ticket punched. I doubt that had I not won that prize, I would have continued as a writer. "Oh, well," I might have thought, "so much for that." Given that experience, why don't I extend the same opportunity to the younger generation that I myself was offered? Whatever my biases, shouldn't I grit my teeth and muster the minimum amount of objectivity required to issue a similar ticket to those following in my footsteps, to give them the same chance? I must admit that, too, makes sense. Perhaps I am to blame for not putting in the effort.

There is, however, another way to think about this. A writer's greatest responsibility is to his readers, to keep providing them with the best work that he is capable of turning out. I am an active writer, which is to say, someone whose work is still in progress. A writer perpetually groping to discover what to do next, inching forward through the perils of the literary battlefield. The task set before me is to survive, and to try and keep moving ahead. Developing the objectivity needed to approve of or reject others' works in a responsible manner, however, sits entirely outside the boundaries of that battlefield. If I were to undertake that new task seriously—and of course that is how it must be done—it would consume no small amount of time and energy. That in turn would cut into the time and energy I have for my own work. To be honest, I don't have that much time to spare. I know that there are others who can manage both, but my hands are full trying to carry out the tasks already on my plate.

Is this egoism? Certainly it's self-centered. I can't argue with that. I simply have to swallow whatever criticism comes my way.

Nevertheless, from what I have seen, publishing houses seem to have no problem putting together juries for their literary prizes. Nor have I heard of publishers forced to terminate a prize for a lack of jury members. To the contrary, from what I can see, the number of prize competitions is only increasing. It feels, in fact, as if someone is being awarded one every day. My failure to serve, it seems, is not causing a social problem by reducing the number of tickets for aspiring writers.

My reluctance stems from another problem, too. Suppose I were to criticize a work under consideration, and someone said to me, "Who are you to be so high and mighty? What about the stuff you have written?" What could I say in reply? I could only agree. I prefer to avoid that situation if at all possible.

Please don't misunderstand—by no means am I denigrating writers (my comrades in arms) who sit on literary prize juries. There are those who are able to focus on their work single-mindedly, while at the same time objectively critiquing works by new writers. They must have a mental switch of some sort that allows them to play that dual role. I can only extend my deepest respect and gratitude to them. Sadly, however, I cannot join their group. I need time to make decisions, and even then, I often make the wrong ones.

I HAVE WRITTEN very little about literary prizes until now. That is because the media tend to play them up irrespective of the quality of the works. Nevertheless, as I said at the outset, that short column about my relationship to the Akutagawa Prize has made me think that the time has come to weigh in on the topic. Otherwise, I fear that a strange misconception might arise that, if left unaddressed, could harden into commonly accepted fact.

It is not as easy as it looks, though, to talk about what that article claims, given its fishy origins and its contentious nature. The more I bare my soul, the less believable—and the more arrogant—I sound. Like a boomerang, my attempt to correct the record could come flying back even faster. When all is said and done, though, I think that honesty is the best policy under the circumstances. For at least some of my readers are sure to believe me.

What I wish to emphasize above all is that a writer's own individual qualities are their most important possession. A literary prize should indirectly reinforce those qualities and not be considered a form of compensation. Still less should it be taken to sum up who the writer is. If the prize manages to reinforce the writer's capacity in a positive way, then it is a "good prize"—if it doesn't, or if it interferes with the writer's work or becomes a burden, then unfortunately it can no longer be called a "good prize." Hence Algren threw away his medal and Chandler was prepared to turn down a trip to Stockholm (though I can't know if he would have followed through on that had he actually won the Nobel).

Literary prizes thus mean vastly different things to different people. Their significance depends on an individual's standpoint, on the writer's circumstances and the way he thinks and lives. You can't lump us all together. That is really all I want to say on the topic of literary prizes. You can't make sweeping statements about them, one way or another. *So you should avoid that, too!*

Not that what I have asserted here is likely to change things in any real way.

On Originality

WHAT IS ORIGINALITY?

That's a hard question to answer. When we say that a work of art is "original," what exactly do we mean? What are its qualifications? These kinds of questions only make us more and more confused when we try to answer them head-on.

The noted neurologist and author Oliver Sacks had this to say about originality, in his essay "Prodigies" from the book *An Anthropologist on Mars:*

> Creativity, as usually understood, entails not only a "what," a talent, but a "who"—strong personal characteristics, a strong identity, personal sensibility, a personal style, which flow into the talent, interfuse it, give it personal body and form. Creativity in this sense involves the power to originate, to break away from the existing ways of looking at things, to move freely in the realm of the imagination, to create and re-create worlds fully in one's mind—while supervising all this with a critical inner eye.[1]

This is a profound definition, precise and to the point. Yet laying it out this way seems to leave something unsaid . . . I can only fold my arms and wonder.

Perhaps the concept of "originality" can be understood more easily if we set direct definitions and rational theories aside and look instead at concrete examples. I remember, for example, the thrill I felt on first hearing the music of the Beatles—I think it was "Please Please Me" on the radio when I was fifteen. I have never forgotten how I felt at that moment. Why such a strong reaction? Well, I had never heard a sound like that, on top of which it was just so *cool*. It's hard to put into words why I found it so wonderful, but it totally blew my mind. I had felt much the same thing a year earlier the first time I heard the Beach Boys sing "Surfin' U.S.A." "Wow!" I had thought. "This is amazing, not like anything else I've heard!"

Looking back, it was the originality of these groups that enthralled me. Their sound was new, their music different than what anyone else was doing, and its quality was far and away the best. They had something special. Something even a fourteen- or fifteen-year-old kid clutching a dinky AM transistor radio with crummy sound could instantly understand. It was that simple.

Far less simple is articulating that difference. In fact, nothing could be more difficult. There's no way I could have done it back then, and even now, as a professional wordsmith, it taxes my linguistic abilities. A somewhat technical approach is required—yet too analytical an explanation can't tell the whole story. It's faster to listen to the music. Your ears will tell!

Nevertheless, more than a half century has passed since the Beatles and Beach Boys came on the scene. It is hard for anyone today to comprehend how powerful the impact of their music was for those of us who experienced it when it was first released.

Naturally, those sounds influenced so many of the musicians who came after. Now everyone takes the music of the Beatles and the Beach Boys for granted. If a fifteen-year-old boy were to hear the same music for the first time today, he might find it amazing, but it is doubtful it would strike him as "unprecedented" in the same dramatic way.

The same thing could be said of *The Rite of Spring* by Igor Stravinsky. When the work was first performed in Paris in 1913, pandemonium broke out—the audience simply couldn't handle that degree of novelty. The music was so unconventional it staggered them. As the number of performances mounted, however, the chaos subsided, so that today *The Rite of Spring* is a popular staple in the classical repertoire. Today we shake our heads in wonder at what could have caused such a ruckus a century ago. Why was the audience so shaken by its "originality"? We can only imagine.

Examples like these might lead us to assume that "originality" is bound to fade with the passage of time, but that is not necessarily the case. Although its initial impact may lessen, it often happens that a work of great quality, if Lady Luck smiles on it, is elevated to the status of "classic" (or semiclassic) once people have become accustomed to it. Once this takes place, respect and admiration for the work becomes even more widespread. Although *The Rite of Spring* may not disconcert modern listeners as it did its original audience, it still feels fresh, and it packs a punch that transcends the historical moment. In fact, the response to Stravinsky's work is internalized as an important touchstone, a resource for the appreciation of music as a whole. It feeds the love of music and contributes to our basic standards of evaluation. One could even make the extreme claim that the depth of a person's musical sensibility can be measured in part by whether or not he or she has listened to *The Rite of Spring*. It may be impossible to measure, but that it has a significant impact on listeners at that level is indisputable.

Gustav Mahler's music presents a slightly different case. It was not properly understood by the people of his time. Most of them—even his contemporaries in the music world—took it to be unpleasant, ugly, loosely constructed, and circuitous. From today's perspective, Mahler can be credited with having undertaken a "deconstruction" of the established symphonic format, but no one looked at his work that way back then. Instead, his fellow musicians belittled his achievement as retrograde and decidedly *unhip*. He owed his musical reputation, in fact, not to his creative work but to his excellence as a conductor. Most of his music was forgotten in the period following his death. Orchestras didn't enjoy performing his works, nor did audiences enjoy listening to them. It was only thanks to a handful of stalwart disciples and devotees, whose determination somehow managed to keep the fire burning, that they continued to be performed at all.

Nevertheless, the popularity of Mahler's music soared dramatically in the 1960s, and his works remain a staple of concert programs. Many people, myself included, find his symphonies thrilling and deeply moving. In short, we have reached back over the years to unearth what we might call Mahler's originality. Such things do happen. Schubert's marvelous piano sonatas, to offer another example, were rarely performed during his lifetime. Only in the latter half of the twentieth century did they find an appreciative audience.

Thelonious Monk is another musician of arresting originality. We—at least those of us interested in jazz—listen to him frequently, so the shock of what he does has largely worn off. We just think,

"Ah, it's Monk," and leave it at that. Yet the originality of his music is clear to anyone who hears it. Its structure and tonal color are totally unlike his contemporaries'. His melodies are unique and played in his own distinctive style. We cannot help responding. For many years, critics didn't give his music proper recognition, but thanks to a small group of avid supporters, people gradually caught on, and today he is widely listened to. In such fashion did the work of Thelonious Monk become an unmistakable and integral part of our internal system of musical cognition. In other words, a classic.

THE SAME PATTERNS characterize the realms of art and literature. Art lovers were shocked, on occasion even repulsed, when they first beheld the paintings of Vincent van Gogh and Pablo Picasso. I doubt many still feel that way. To the contrary, their art is now found to be deeply moving, invigorating, even psychically healing. That's not because it has lost its originality with time; rather, that originality has become one with our perception, so that, naturally, it has become a part of us, a reference point, as it were.

Similarly, the literary styles of Natsume Sōseki and Ernest Hemingway are now celebrated. Yet both were criticized, at times even ridiculed, by their contemporaries. Not a few of their readers (many of whom belonged to the cultural elite at the time) were turned off. Today, however, their styles function as a kind of standard. It is my impression, in fact, that if Sōseki and Hemingway had never developed those styles, the literature that we read today in the West and in Japan would be somewhat different. Taking it a step further, I think it's arguable that their styles have become part of the mental landscapes of Japanese and English readers.

IT IS RELATIVELY EASY to take up examples of "originality" from the past and analyze them from today's perspective. Almost always, the things that should have disappeared—for lack of originality—have already done so, leaving us to confidently evaluate what remains. As countless instances show, however, it is far more difficult to properly assess, in real time, new forms of expression in our immediate environment. That is because they often contain elements seen as unpleasant, unnatural, nonsensical, or sometimes even antisocial. Or else just plain stupid. Whatever the case, those around us tend to react with surprise and, at the same time, shock. People instinctively dislike those things they can't understand, a pattern characteristic of members of the establishment who are buried up to their ears in the dominant forms of expression. They tend to apprehend the newcomer with abhorrence and disgust, because, in a worst-case scenario, the very ground upon which they stand might fall away from under them.

The Beatles would seem to occupy a special category, since they were popular from the outset, thanks to their huge base of youthful fans. Yet that popularity was far from universal. Many saw their songs as no more than a passing fad, throwaway music not in the same league with classic works. In fact, most of the establishment actively disliked them and expressed that disapproval every chance they got. It's hard to believe now, but many older people detested their haircuts and fashion, to the point that it became a social problem. There were even scattered demonstrations where Beatles records were gleefully broken or torched. Only later did the general public come to appreciate how innovative, and how good, their music was. In other words, only when it had achieved "classic" status.

In his early days, Bob Dylan played the acoustic guitar and sang protest songs, carrying on the tradition of Woody Guthrie and Pete Seeger. When he abandoned that style and went electric, however, a great number of his supporters raked him over the coals, cursing him as a "Judas" and a "traitor" for selling out to commercialism. Yet almost no one comments on that move today. In fact, if we listen to his records in chronological sequence, it becomes clear that they represent the natural and necessary evolution of a creative spirit engaged in a constant process of self-reinvention. To those who at the time tried to cage his originality within the narrow category of "protest folk singer," though, he was no more than a treacherous infidel.

The Beach Boys were a great hit as a working band, but the heavy pressure to produce original material affected the nerves of their musical leader, Brian Wilson, to such a degree that he essentially retreated into isolation, where he remained for many years. The intricately constructed works that followed his masterpiece, *Pet Sounds*, deeply disappointed his fan base, who were hoping for something closer to the happy surfing sound of his early career. Yet his music became progressively complex and difficult. I confess that I am one of those who drifted away from the Beach Boys during this time—I just couldn't understand what they were getting at. Now, I can appreciate the direction they were moving in and how wonderful the music is, but at the time, I honestly couldn't. "Originality" is a living, evolving thing, whose shape is devilishly hard to pin down.

I N   M Y   O P I N I O N , an artist must fulfill the following three basic requirements to be deemed "original":

1. The artist must possess a clearly unique and individual style (of sound, language, or color). Moreover, that uniqueness should be immediately perceivable on first sight (or hearing).
2. That style must have the power to update itself. It should grow with time, never resting in the same place for long, since it expresses an internal and spontaneous process of self-reinvention.
3. Over time, that characteristic style should become integrated within the psyche of its audience, to become a part of their basic standard of evaluation. Subsequent generations of artists should see that style as a rich resource from which they can draw.

An artist need not fulfill all three requirements equally, of course, to be considered "original." There are cases where requirements 1 and 3 are clear while 2 is a little weak, or where 2 and 3 are clear while 1 is somehow lacking. Nevertheless, it is fair to say that the basic components of "originality" can, to a greater or lesser degree, be found within these boundaries.

Setting 1 aside for the time being, we can see that, for both 2 and 3, the passage of time is a significant element. In short, whether a creator and his or her work qualify as original or not depends to a large part on the test of time. When an artist with a unique style grabs the eyes or ears of the public and then vanishes from sight or grows tiresome, it's hard to call them "original." Rather, they're more likely to fall into the "flash in the pan" category.

I have witnessed that pattern in a variety of fields. Creative artists may grab your attention right off the bat with their daring novelty, but before you know it, they have disappeared. At some point thereafter, they become one of those people you think of only to wonder, "Whatever happened to so-and-so?" Artists of that sort probably lack staying power and a capacity for self-reinvention. Before we can say much about an artist's style, we need to see an accumulated body of work. Otherwise there just isn't enough to go on. We can't really assess someone's originality until we can line up a number of their works and examine them from a variety of angles.

Suppose, for example, that Beethoven had composed only one symphony in his life—the Ninth. How then would we evaluate him as a composer? Could we deduce the Ninth's intrinsic significance, or its degree of originality, in isolation? I think it would be very difficult. Looking at his symphonies alone, I think it is only because we are able to see the Ninth as a continuation from the First through the Eighth that we can fathom the Ninth's greatness, and its overwhelming originality, in a three-dimensional and contextualized way.

I hope to be "original" in my expression, just as I imagine all artists do. As I have already explained, however, it's not something I myself can determine. However loudly I proclaim it from the rooftops, however often I am praised for it by the critics and the media, our voices are fated to vanish in the wind. All I can do is entrust the final decision to those for whom I write—in other words, my readers—and the passage of an appropriate amount of time. My sole task is to work as hard as I can to provide as many "cases" as possible. In short, to keep adding works I can be satisfied with to the pile, buttressing and extending my total oeuvre.

One saving grace—or at least a possible salvation—for me is the fact that so many literary critics have harshly criticized my works. One famous critic has even branded me a "con man." I guess by that he means that I have been swindling my readers by feeding them meaningless drivel. Since a novelist is, to some extent, an illusionist by trade, I suppose being called a con man may be taken as a kind of reverse compliment, in which case maybe I should rejoice at being attacked in those terms. Still, to be honest, having someone say those things about me—or, more precisely, write them down on paper for public consumption—isn't a lot of fun. An illusionist is, after all, an occupation of sorts, while marriage fraud is a crime, which makes me feel the expression is rather lacking in delicacy. (Then again, perhaps the problem is not an absence of delicacy but a sloppy choice of metaphor.)

There were members of the literary community, of course, who looked favorably on my work, but they were few and their voices were lost in the din. Overall, in my estimation, the nos emanating from the literary establishment outweighed the yeses by a wide margin. In those days, if I had leapt into a pond to save an old woman from drowning, the critics—and I mean this only half-jokingly—would have found something to carp about. "A mere publicity stunt," they would have scoffed. "Surely she could have swum to shore."

At the beginning, when I was still uncertain if my work was any good, I tended to take the criticism to heart, though I tried to shrug it off, but as time passed I gained a *certain amount* of confidence— never more than a certain amount, mind you—that my novels were turning out well. Nevertheless, the storm of criticism showed no signs of abating. To the contrary, the gusts only grew stronger. I came to feel like a tennis player whose ball is blown away every time he tosses it up to serve.

It seems there's a sizable number of critics who will go on disliking whatever I write, no matter its quality. The fact that my form of expression rubs them the wrong way doesn't necessarily mean that my writing is original, of course. That goes without saying. Generally speaking, the works dismissed by critics as unpleasant or faulty are just that. Yet that leaves open the *possibility* that their reaction also fulfills one of the requirements of true originality. Or at least this is what, when a critic savaged my work, I told myself, trying to be as positive as possible. Better to evoke a strong response, even a negative one, than to elicit nothing but humdrum comments and lukewarm praise.

The Polish poet Zbigniew Herbert had this to say: "To reach the source, you have to swim against the current. Only trash swims downstream."[2] Lines like these can really buck up your spirits!

I'm not a big fan of generalizations, but if you will permit me to venture one (my apologies!), Japan is a country where most people really hate it when you go against the flow. For better or for worse, our culture places an extreme emphasis on harmony, which means that Japanese care way too much about "making waves." To put it another way, the social and political framework of Japan tends to stiffen very quickly, making it that much easier for authority to throw its weight around.

In the case of literature, for a long time after the Second World War ended, the literary status of authors and their works was carefully arranged and slotted within an axis of fixed coordinates— "vanguard" vs. "rear guard," "right wing" vs. "left wing," "popular" vs. "serious." At the same time, the big publishing houses (almost all of which were based in Tokyo) set the tone for what was considered good literature through their literary magazines, a set of standards that was confirmed by a system of prizes (or "goodies") for authors. It was very hard to stand against this monolithic system. Leaving the axis meant forgoing all the goodies that were being passed around.

When I made my debut as a writer in 1979, this system was still firmly entrenched, its power basically unchallenged. Editors would say things like "There's no precedent for that" or "That's just not the way things are done." It had been my impression that one thing an author had going for him was that he was free to write whatever he wanted, so comments like these truly puzzled me.

I'm not the type of guy who enjoys fighting and arguing (really!), so I wasn't up for battling the system, or duking it out with any of the unwritten laws. I am, however, an independent person who likes to think things out for himself. Having taken the trouble to become a writer, and realizing that we all get only one chance in this life, I was determined from the start to forge ahead and do what I wanted in the way I wanted. The system could go its way and I would go mine. As someone who had lived through the student protests of the late 1960s, the years of rebellion, it went against my instincts to "sell out" to those in power. Most of all, however, as a writer I wanted to remain spiritually free, beholden to no one. To write my novels the way I wanted, according to the schedule I myself had laid out. This was my bottom line, my assertion of authorial independence.

From the outset, I had a pretty clear idea of the novels I wanted to create. I could even picture *what they should look like*, once I had developed my skills to the point where I could write them.

The novels floated directly above me, shining in the sky like the North Star. If I felt lost, all I had to do was look up. They would give me my location, and point me in the right direction. Had they not been there, I might well have ended up wandering all over the place.

Speaking from experience, it seems that I discovered my "original" voice and style, at the outset, not adding to what I already knew but *subtracting* from it. Think how many—far too many— things we pick up in the course of living. Whether we choose to call it information overload or excess baggage, we have that multitude of options to choose from, so that when we try to express ourselves creatively, all those choices collide with each other and we shut down, like a stalled engine. We become paralyzed. Our best recourse is to clear out our information system by chucking all that is unnecessary into the garbage bin, allowing our mind to move freely again.

How, then, can we distinguish between those contents that are crucial, those that are less necessary, and those that are entirely unnecessary?

Speaking again from experience, I have found that these distinctions are actually quite easy to make. One rule of thumb is to ask yourself, "Am I having a good time doing this?" If you're not enjoying yourself when you're engaged in what seems important to you, if you can't find spontaneous pleasure and joy in it, if your heart doesn't leap with excitement, then there's likely something wrong. When that happens, you have to go back to the beginning and start discarding any extraneous parts or unnatural elements.

That can be a lot harder than it sounds.

Right after I won the Gunzo Prize for New Writers for *Hear the Wind Sing*, a high-school classmate of mine stopped by my jazz café to offer his comments on my novel. "If something that simple can make it, I could write a novel, too," he sniffed, and left. I was a little put out, of course, but I also knew what he meant. "The guy may not be entirely off the mark," I thought. "Perhaps anybody could turn out something as good." All I had done was sit down and riff on whatever came into my head. There were no complicated words, no elaborate phrases, no elegant style. I had just thrown it together as I went along. If that classmate of mine did go home and write a novel, however, I never heard about it. Maybe he figured there was no need for him to write in a world where novels as half-baked as mine could pass muster. If so, it probably showed good judgment on his part.

Looking back, however, it strikes me that for an aspiring writer, writing "something that simple" may not be so simple. It's easy enough to think and talk about ridding your mind of unnecessary things through a process of subtraction and simplification, but actually doing it is hard. I think that I was able to pull it off without too much fuss because I had never been obsessed by the idea of being a writer, so I was not hindered by that ambition.

In any event, that was how I began. I started with a simple style, light and breezy, and then took time fleshing it out bit by bit in later works. The structure of my novels, too, was skeletal at first, but I built it up in stages, making it more three-dimensional and multi-layered until it was strong enough to handle the heightened complexity of long narratives. In this fashion, my works grew in scale. As I said before, I began with an internal image of what I eventually wanted to write, but the process of getting there happened naturally. No detailed planning was involved—only after I had arrived did it hit me, "So that's how I got here!"

If there is indeed something original about my novels, I think it springs from the principle of freedom. I had just turned twenty-nine when, for no particular reason, I thought, "I feel like writing a novel!" so I sat down and started. I had never planned to be a writer and had never given serious thought to what sort of novel I should be writing, which meant that I was under no particular constraints. I hadn't the slightest idea what was taking place in the literary world in Japan, and (for better or for worse) I had no older author to look up to as a role model. I just wanted to write something that reflected what I was feeling at the time—nothing more. It was that simple, straightforward impulse that drove me to start scribbling, without a thought to what might lie ahead. There was no need to feel self-conscious. In fact, writing was fun—it let me feel free and natural.

I think (or hope) that free and natural sensibility lies at the heart of my novels. That is what has spurred me to write. My engine, as it were. It is my belief that a rich, spontaneous joy lies at the root of all creative expression. What is originality, after all, but the *shape* that results from the natural impulse to communicate to others that feeling of freedom, that unconstrained joy?

Perhaps pure impulse brings with it its own form and style in a natural, involuntary way. Form and style are, in that sense, far from artificial. A brilliant person may use every ounce of his intelligence to develop form and style, may diagram every step, but if he lacks that natural impulse he is likely to fail or, if not fail, produce something that will not last. It will be like a plant whose roots are not firmly set in the earth: if there is too little rain it will lose its vitality and wither, while if it rains too hard it will be swept away with the topsoil.

THIS IS PURELY MY OPINION, but if you want to express yourself as freely as you can, it's probably best not to start out by asking "What am I seeking?" Rather, it's better to ask "Who would I be if I weren't seeking anything?" and then try to visualize that aspect of yourself. Asking "What am I seeking?" invariably leads you to ponder heavy issues. The heavier that discussion gets, the farther freedom retreats, and the slower your footwork becomes. The slower your footwork, the less lively your prose. When that happens, your writing won't charm anyone—possibly even you.

The you who is not seeking anything, by contrast, is as light and free as a butterfly. All you have to do is uncup your hands and let it soar. Your words will flow effortlessly. People normally don't concern themselves with self-expression—they just live their lives. Yet, *despite that*, you want to say something. Perhaps it is in the natural context of "despite that" where we unexpectedly catch sight of something essential about ourselves.

I have been writing fiction for more than thirty-five years at the time of this book's writing; yet I have never experienced what is commonly known as "writer's block." Wanting to write but being unable to is unknown to me. That may make it sound as if I am overflowing with talent, but the actual reason is much simpler: I never write unless I really want to, unless the desire to write is overwhelming. When I feel that desire, I sit down and set to work. When I don't feel it, I usually turn to translating from English. Since translation is essentially a technical operation, I can pursue it on a daily basis, quite separate from my creative desire; yet at the same time it is a good way to hone my writing skills—were I not a translator, I'm sure I would have found another related pursuit. If I am in the mood, I may also turn to writing essays. "What the heck," I defiantly tell myself as I peck away at those other projects. "Not writing novels isn't going to kill me."

After a while, however, the desire to write begins to mount. I can feel my material building up within me, like spring melt pressing against a dam. Then one day (in a best-case scenario), when I can't take that pressure anymore, I sit down at my desk and start to write. Worry about journal editors impatiently awaiting a promised manuscript never enters the picture. I don't make promises, so I don't have deadlines. As a result, writer's block and I are strangers to each other. As you might expect, that makes my life much happier. It must be terribly stressful for a writer to be put in the position of having to write when he doesn't feel like it. (Could I be wrong? Do most writers actually thrive on that kind of stress?)

RETURNING TO WHERE we started, when I think about "originality" I am transported back to my boyhood days. I can see myself in my room sitting in front of my little transistor radio listening for the first time to the Beach Boys ("Surfin' U.S.A.") and the Beatles ("Please Please Me"). "Wow!" I'm thinking. "This is fantastic! I've never heard anything like this!" I am so moved. It is as if their music has thrown open a new window in my soul, and air of a kind I have never breathed before is pouring in. I feel a sense of profound well-being, a natural high. Liberated from the constraints of reality, it is as if my feet have left the ground. This to me is how "originality" should feel: pure and simple.

I came across this line recently in *The New York Times*, written about the American debut of the Beatles: "They produced a sound that was fresh, energetic and unmistakably their own." These words may provide the best definition of originality available. "Fresh, energetic, and unmistakably your own."

Originality is hard to define in words, but it is possible to describe and reproduce the emotional state it evokes. I try to attain that emotional state each time I sit down to write my novels. That's because it feels so wonderfully invigorating. It's as if a new and different day is being born from the day that is today.

If possible, I would like my readers to savor that same emotion when they read my books. I want to open a window in their souls and let the fresh air in. This is what I think of, and hope for, as I write—purely and simply.

So What Should I Write About?

WHEN I DO Q&A sessions with young people, they often ask me what it takes to become a novelist—what kinds of training, what sorts of personal habits. This question seems to arise no matter where I am in the world. I guess it goes to show just how many people there are who want to be writers, to engage in "self-expression"—but all the same, it's a tricky one to answer. At least I have difficulty coming up with a good response.

That's because I myself have a hard time understanding how I made it this far. I didn't have my heart set on becoming a novelist when I was young, nor did I follow a series of steps to earn my spurs—no special studies, no training, no piling up of notebook exercises. Like so many things in my life, events seemed to follow their own course, pulling me along. Luck played a big part, too. It's rather unnerving when I look back now, but there's no way around it—that's the way it was.

Still, when I look around at the earnest faces of young would-be writers asking what they should do to prepare, I can't really say,

"I have no idea. Just let things take their course and hope Lady Luck smiles on you. Pretty scary, when you think about it," and then jump to the next question. That would be too mean. In fact, it could cast a pall over the whole event. As a result, I have attempted to tackle the issue head-on to come up with a proper sort of answer.

So here goes.

I think the first task for the aspiring novelist is to read tons of novels. Sorry to start with such a commonplace observation, but no training is more crucial. To write a novel, you must first understand at a physical level how one is put together. This point is as self-evident as the truism "You can't make an omelet without breaking a few eggs."

It is especially important to plow through as many novels as you can while you are still young. Everything you can get your hands on—great novels, not-so-great novels, crappy novels, it doesn't matter (at all!) as long as you keep reading. Absorb as many stories as you physically can. Introduce yourself to lots of great writing. To lots of mediocre writing, too. This is your most important task. Through it you will develop the basic novelistic muscles that every novelist needs. Build up your foundation. Make it strong while you have time to spare and while your eyes are still good. Writing is important, too, I guess, but it can come later—there is no need to rush.

Next, before you start writing your own stuff, make a habit of looking at things and events in more detail. Observe what is going on around you and the people you encounter as closely and as deeply as you can. Reflect on what you see. Remember, though, that to reflect is not to rush to determine the rights and wrongs or merits and demerits of what and whom you are observing. Try to consciously refrain from value judgments—conclusions can come later. What's important is not arriving at clear conclusions but retaining the specifics of a certain situation—in other words, your material—as fully as you can.

Some individuals decide what or who is right or wrong based on a quick analysis of people and events. Generally speaking, though (and this is purely my opinion), they don't make good novelists. Instead, they are better suited to becoming critics or journalists. Or possibly academics of a certain kind. Someone cut out to be a novelist, on the other hand, will stop to question the conclusion he or she has just reached, or is about to reach. "It sure looks that way," he or she will think, "but wait a minute. That might be only my preconceived notion. Maybe I should consider it more carefully. After all, things are never as simple as they seem. If down the road something new pops up, it could become a completely different story."

That's the type of guy I seem to be. Of course, my brain doesn't work that fast in the first place, so when I do voice a quick opinion on something it often turns out to be wrong (or inadequate, or completely off the mark), a failing that has led me into countless painful experiences. Over and over again, I have been embarrassed, or put in a tight spot, or sent off on a fool's errand. As a result, little by little, I have developed the habit of questioning my immediate response to things. This pattern of behavior is not natural to me; rather, it is acquired, the result of a long list of disastrous decisions.

That is why I don't leap to judgment when something happens. My mind no longer works that way. Instead I strive to retain as complete an image as possible of the scene I have observed, the person I have met, the experience I have undergone, regarding it as a singular "sample," a kind of test case, as it were. I can go back and look at it again later, when my feelings have settled down and there is less urgency, this time inspecting it from a variety of angles. Finally, if and when it seems called for, I can draw my own conclusions.

Nevertheless, based on my own experience, I have found that the occasions when conclusions must be drawn are far less numerous than we tend to assume. Indeed, the times when judgments are *truly* necessary—whether in the short or the long run—are few and far between. That's the way I feel, anyway. This means that when I read the paper or watch the news on TV, I have a hard time swallowing the reporters' rush to give opinions on anything and everything. "Come on, guys," I feel like saying, "what's the big hurry?"

There is a general expectation in the world today that choices should be laid out in black-and-white terms as quickly as possible. Of course, some questions must be answered right away. To take a couple of extreme examples, "Should we go to war?" and "Should we restart our nuclear reactors tomorrow?" require us to take clear and prompt positions. If we don't, then all hell could break loose. Yet occasions like those, which compel us to come to a firm decision, are not all that frequent. When less time is taken between gathering information and acting on it, so that everyone becomes a critic or a news commentator, then the world becomes an edgier, less reflective place. And probably much more dangerous, too. Opinion surveys allow you to check the box "Undecided." Well, I think there should be another box you can check: "Undecided *at the present time*."

Enough talk about today's world—let's get back to the aspiring novelist. As I have said, the challenge is not to form value judgments but, rather, to stockpile as much material as possible in its original form. To create an inner space in which it can all be stored.

Of course, realistically, it is impossible to retain everything. There is a limit to how much our memory can hold. Thus, we need a minimal kind of information-processing system to reduce the amount.

In most cases, I try to fix a few telling details about the event (or the person, or the scene) in my mind. Since it is hard to recall (or, having attempted to remember, easy to forget) the whole picture, it is best to try to extract specific features in a form that can be easily held for safekeeping. This is what I mean by a minimal system.

What sorts of features? They tend to be those striking details that make you sit up straight, that fix themselves in your mind. Ideally, those things that can't be explained away. It is best if they are illogical, or counter the flow of events in a subtle way, or tempt you to question them, or suggest some kind of mystery. You gather these bits, affix a simple label (place, time, situation) and mentally file them away in your personal chest of drawers. It is possible, of course, to jot them down on a notepad or something of the sort, but I prefer to trust my mind. It's a real pain to carry a pad around, and I have found that once I have jotted something down I tend to relax and forget it. If I toss the bits into my mind, on the other hand, what needs to be remembered stays while the rest fades into oblivion. I like to leave things to this process of natural selection.

This reminds me of an anecdote I'm fond of. When Paul Valéry was interviewing Albert Einstein, he asked the great scientist, "Do you carry a notebook around to record your ideas?" Einstein was an unflappable man, but this question clearly unnerved him. "No," he answered. "There's no need for that. You see I rarely have new ideas."

Come to think of it, there have been very few situations when I wished I had a notepad on me. Something truly important is not that easy to forget once you've entrusted it to your memory.

YOUR MENTAL CHEST OF DRAWERS is a great asset when you set to work on a novel. Neatly put-together arguments and value judgments aren't much use for those of us who write fiction. More often than not, they impede us by blocking the natural flow of the story. If you have stockpiled your chest with a rich variety of unrelated details, however, you will be amazed to see how naturally they pop up when the need arises, full of life and ready to be fit into the narrative.

So what sorts of details am I talking about?

Let me think. Okay, let's say you know someone who for no apparent reason starts sneezing when they get really angry. Once the sneezing fit begins, it goes on and on. Now, I don't know anyone like that, but for the sake of argument, let's say you do. What, you wonder, explains this pattern? One approach would be to try to come up with a tentative theory—physiological, perhaps, or psychological—to analyze their behavior. My brain, however, doesn't work that way. I think, "Wow, people like that exist," and leave it at that. Instead of drawing an inference, I take it as an example of the variety of things in the world, filing it away as an undifferentiated lump. The drawers of my mental chest are full of disjointed memories of this sort that I have collected and stored.

James Joyce put it most succinctly when he said, "Imagination is memory." I tend to agree with him. In fact, I think he was spot-on. What we call the imagination consists of fragments of memory that lack any clear connection with one another. This may sound like a contradiction in terms, but when we bring such fragments together our intuition is sparked, and we sense what the future may hold in store. It is from their interaction that a novel's true power emanates.

We are—or at least I am—equipped with this expansive mental chest of drawers. Each drawer is packed with memories, or information. There are big drawers and small ones. A few have secret compartments, where information can be hidden. When I am writing, I can open them, extract the material I need, and add it to my story. Their numbers are countless, but when I am focused on my writing I know without thinking exactly which drawer holds what and can immediately put my hands on what I am looking for. Memories I could never recall otherwise come naturally to me. It's a great feeling to enter into this elastic, unrestrained state, as if my imagination had pulled free from my thinking mind to function as an autonomous, independent entity. Needless to say, for a novelist like me the information stored in my chest is a rich and irreplaceable resource.

In Steven Soderbergh's film *Kafka,* Jeremy Irons, in the lead role, sneaks into a creepy castle (based, of course, on *The Castle*) through a cabinet filled with rows of drawers. When I saw that scene, it struck me that it looked like a spatial representation of my own brain. It's a really interesting film, so check out that scene if you get the chance. My brain isn't quite that creepy, but the structure may be similar.

ALTHOUGH I COMPOSE essays as well as works of fiction, unless circumstances dictate otherwise I avoid working on anything else when I am writing a novel. That's because if I am turning out a series of essays and I dip into one of my memory drawers, I may extract material that I need later. That may mean I open a drawer to get something for my novel only to discover that it has already appeared somewhere else. If I want to include the story of someone who starts sneezing whenever they get angry, for example, but have already published it in a weekly journal, it can be a real disappointment. Of course, there is no rule that says that the same material can't be used in an essay and a story, but I have found that doubling up like that somehow weakens my fiction. My advice, then, is to hang a sign on your chest of drawers that says For Fiction Only when you are in the process of writing. You never know what you are going to need later, so it pays to be miserly. This is one piece of wisdom I have picked up in the course of my long career.

When you emerge from the novel-writing process, you can dip into the unopened drawers, take the unused material (what might be called "surplus goods") stored there, and use it in your essays. In my case, though, essays are no more than a sideline, like the cans of oolong tea marketed by beer companies. If something is really tasty, I save it for my main job—my next novel. Once a critical mass of such material has accumulated, my desire to launch a new book naturally kicks in. This is why I guard my chest of drawers so carefully.

Remember the scene in Steven Spielberg's film *E.T.* where E.T. assembles a transmitting device from the junk he pulls out of the garage? There's an umbrella, a floor lamp, pots and pans, a record player—it's been a long time since I saw the movie, so I can't recall everything, but he manages to throw all those household items together in such a way that the contraption works well enough to communicate with his home planet thousands of light years away. I got a big kick out of that scene when I saw it in the movie theater, but it strikes me now that putting together a good novel is much the same thing. The key component is not the quality of the materials—what's needed is *magic*. If that magic is present, the most basic daily matters and the plainest language can be turned into a device of surprising sophistication.

First and foremost, though, is what's packed away in your garage. Magic can't work if your garage is empty. You've got to stash away a lot of junk to use if and when E.T. comes calling!

T H E   F I R S T   T I M E I sat down to write a novel, nothing came to mind—I was completely stumped. I hadn't been through a war like my parents, or endured the postwar chaos and hunger of the generation directly above me. I had no experience of revolution (I had experienced a kind of ersatz revolution but didn't want to write about that), nor had I undergone any form of brutal abuse or discrimination that I could remember. Instead I had grown up in a typical middle-class home in a peaceful suburban community, where I suffered no particular want, and although my life had been far from perfect, neither was it steeped in misfortune (in relative terms I was fortunate). In other words, I had spent a mundane and nondescript youth. My grades weren't the greatest, but they weren't the worst, either. There was nothing, in short, that I felt absolutely compelled to write about. I possessed some measure of desire to express myself, but had no *intrinsic* topic at hand. As a result, until I turned twenty-nine I never considered writing a novel of my own. I lacked material, I thought, as well as the talent to create something without it. I was someone who could only read novels. And read them I did, piles and piles of them, never supposing for a moment that I could write one.

I believe that the younger generation today faces quite similar circumstances. In fact, they may have even fewer issues that beg to be written about than we did. What, then, to do under such circumstances?

The way I see it, the "E.T. method" is their sole option. Their only recourse is to throw open their garage doors, drag out whatever they have stored away to that point—even if it looks like no more than a pile of useless junk—and slave away until the magic takes hold. No other approach can help us contact distant planets. We can only try our best with what we have at hand. If you do give it your best shot, though, success can be yours. You can realize the glorious feeling of *practicing magic.* For writing a novel is in the end forging a link with people on other planets. For real!

WHEN I BEGAN my first novel, *Hear the Wind Sing,* I knew I had no choice but to write about *having nothing to write about.* That I would somehow have to turn having nothing to write about into a weapon if I was going to move forward as a novelist. Otherwise I would be powerless to stand against the generation of writers who had preceded me. This, I think, is an example of what writing with what you have at hand implies.

Adopting this approach requires new language and a new style. You have to fashion a vehicle that no one has driven before. Since you won't—can't—handle heavy topics like war, revolution, and famine, you must deal with lighter material, which in turn impels you to develop a lighter vehicle that is agile and mobile.

After a great deal of trial and error—I will save the details of this process for another occasion—I was able to cobble together an appropriate Japanese style to use in my work. It was far from perfect, with holes scattered here and there, but I figured it was my first novel, so I had to accept it as it was. I could fix the mistakes the next time around—if there was a next time.

Two principles guided me. The first was to omit all explanations. Instead, I would toss a variety of fragments—episodes, images, scenes, phrases—into that container called the novel and then try to join them together in a three-dimensional way. Second, I would try to make those connections in a space set entirely apart from conventional logic and literary clichés. This was my basic scheme.

More than anything else, music helped move this process forward. I wrote as if I were performing a piece of music. Jazz was my main inspiration. As you know, the most important aspect of a jazz performance is rhythm. You have to sustain a solid rhythm from start to finish—when you fail, people stop listening. The next most important element is the chords, or harmony if you like. Beautiful chords, muddy chords, secondary chords, chords with the tonic removed. Bud Powell's chords, Thelonious Monk's chords, Bill Evans's chords, Herbie Hancock's chords. There are so many kinds. Though everyone is using a piano with the same eighty-eight keys, the sound varies to an amazing degree depending on who's playing. This says something important about novel writing as well. The possibilities are limitless—or virtually limitless—even if we use the same limited material. The fact that a piano has only eighty-eight keys hardly means that nothing new can be done with it.

Finally there is the matter of free improvisation, which lies at the root of jazz music. Once the rhythm and chord progression (or harmonic structure) have been established, the musician is able to weave notes freely into the composition.

I can't play a musical instrument. Or at least I can't play one well enough to expect people to listen to me. Yet I have the strong desire to perform music. From the beginning, therefore, my intention was to write as if I were playing an instrument. I still feel like that today. I sit tapping away at the keyboard searching for the right rhythm, the most suitable chords and tones. This is, and has always been, the most important element in my literature.

IN MY OPINION (and this is based on my experience), having nothing you feel compelled to write about may make it harder to get started, but once the engine kicks in and the vehicle starts rolling, the writing is actually easier. This is because the flip side of having nothing you must write is being able to write freely about anything. Your material may be lightweight, but if you can grasp how to link the pieces together so that magic results, you can go on to write as many novels as you wish. You will be astounded how the mastery of that technique can lead to the creation of works with both weight and depth—as long as, that is, you retain a healthy amount of writerly ambition.

In contrast, writers who from the first write about heavy topics may eventually—although, obviously, this does not occur in all cases—find themselves faltering under the very weight of that material. Writers who launch their careers writing about war, for example, can approach their subject matter from various angles in various works, but at a certain point they may, to some degree or other, find themselves backed into a corner when forced to think of what to write next. Some are able to continue to grow as novelists by shifting course in midcareer. Those who are unable to accomplish this change of direction, however, may sadly find their strength waning over time.

Ernest Hemingway, without a doubt one of the most influential writers of the twentieth century, is widely considered to have produced his greatest work early in his career. I especially like his two early novels, *The Sun Also Rises* and *A Farewell to Arms*, as well as his early Nick Adams stories. These are all written with breathtaking vigor. Yet his later works, while brilliant in part, fail to realize their potential and lack the stylistic freshness of his earlier writing. In my opinion, this falloff likely stemmed from the fact that Hemingway was the type of writer who took his strength from his material. This helps explain why he led the type of life he did, moving from one war to another (the First World War, the Spanish Civil War, the Second World War), hunting big game in Africa, fishing for big fish, falling in love with bullfighting. He needed that external stimulus to write. The result was a legendary life; yet age gradually sapped him of the energy that his experiences had once provided. This is pure conjecture, but my guess is that it helps to explain why Hemingway, after winning the Nobel Prize for Literature in 1954, sank into alcoholism and then took his own life in 1961, at the very height of his fame.

WRITERS WHO DO NOT rely on weighty material but instead reach inside themselves to spin their tales may, by contrast, have an easier time of it. That's because they can draw on their daily lives—the events routinely taking place around them, the scenes they witness, the people they encounter—and then freely apply their imaginations to that material to construct their own fiction. In short, they use a form of renewable energy. They feel no need to fight on the battlefield or in the bullring, or to shoot lions.

Please do not misunderstand—I am not saying that direct personal involvement in things like war, bullfights, and big-game hunting has no meaning. Of course it can be meaningful. Experiences are crucial for a writer, of whatever kind. All I'm saying is that they needn't be of the dramatic variety to make a good novel. Even the smallest, most nondramatic encounter can generate an astonishing amount of creative power, if you do it right.

There is a saying in Japanese, "When trees sink and rocks float." It refers to occurrences that contravene the norm; but in the world of the novel—or perhaps, more broadly, in the realm of art—such reversals take place all the time. Things the world sees as trivial can acquire weight over time, while other things broadly considered to be weighty can, quite suddenly, reveal themselves to be only hollow shells. The unending creative process cannot be perceived by the naked eye, but its power, aided by the passing of time, yields such drastic turnarounds on a regular basis.

So if you lament that you lack the material you need to write, you are giving up way too easily. If you just shift your focus a little bit and slightly alter your way of thinking, you will discover a wealth of material lying about just waiting to be picked up and used. You only have to look. In the field of human endeavor, things that seem mundane at first glance can, if you persevere, give birth to an endless array of insights. All you need to do, as I said before, is retain your healthy writerly ambition. That is the key.

I HAVE LONG HELD that no generation is superior or inferior to another. Although stereotypes about age groups being better or worse are common, I am convinced such criticisms don't hold water. Generations should never be ranked that way. Of course each has its own tendencies. But there are no differences in the quantity or quality of talent. At least not enough to matter.

To take one concrete example, today's Japanese youth are often criticized for being poorer at reading and writing kanji than their elders. (I have no idea whether this is true or not.) At the same time, however, there is little doubt that they are far better at understanding and processing computer language. This is exactly my point. Each generation has its own deficiencies as well as its own fields of expertise. It's that simple. Correspondingly, each generation should stress its respective strengths in its creative activities. Writers should use their own language as a weapon, choosing words that come naturally to them to depict what they see as clearly as they can. There is no need for them to be intimidated by their elders; nor, on the other side of the coin, do they have any justification for feeling superior.

I took a lot of heat when I launched my career. "This can't be called a novel," older critics fumed. "This isn't literature!" I found the constant attacks quite depressing, so I left Japan for a number of years and went to live abroad, where I could write what I wanted in peace, free of the constant static. Never, though, did I entertain serious misgivings about my approach or feel particularly anxious about what I was doing. "I can't write any other way, so take it or leave it," was my response to the critics. My writing still isn't perfect, but I was sure even then that if I kept at it, I could turn out something better. I was convinced that I was following the correct path and that the value of my work would become apparent with the passing of time. I sure had a lot of nerve!

Now, when I look around me, I can't be sure whether I've been proven right or not. How can I possibly tell? I doubt that literary value can ever be fully gauged, however much time passes. Nevertheless, my belief that I am basically headed in the right direction has remained unshaken since 1979, when I published my first novel. In another three or four decades, conditions will have changed yet again and the situation will be clearer, but given my age, I may not be around to see for myself. I hope one of you can keep an eye on things for me.

IN THE END, I think each new generation has its own fixed amount of material that it can use to write novels, and that the shape and relative weight of that material retroactively determine the shape and function of the vehicle that must be designed to carry it. It is from the correlation of material and vehicle—from their interface, as it were—that new forms of novelistic reality emerge.

Every era, every generation, experiences its own "reality." The novelist's job of painstakingly collecting and stockpiling that material is as crucial as ever, and will remain so in the future.

So if your aim is to write fiction, take a close look around you. The world may appear a mundane place, but in fact it is filled with a variety of enigmatic and mysterious ores. Novelists are people who happen to have the knack of discovering and refining that raw material. Even more wonderful: the process costs virtually nothing. If you are blessed with a pair of good eyes, you too can mine the ore you choose to your heart's content!

Can you think of a more wonderful way to make a living?

Making Time Your Ally:
On Writing a Novel

↳

N MY MANY YEARS as a professional writer, I have written works of varying sizes in a wide variety of literary forms.
Extremely long novels (*1Q84*, for example), slim novels (like
After Dark), short stories, even shorter "palm of the hand" stories,
and so on. If I were to compare these to naval vessels, they would
run the gamut from aircraft carriers to destroyers to submarines,
covering all the boats in the navy (not that there is warlike intent
in anything I write!). Each ship has its own purposes, its own role:
they are designed so that one complements the others. And so it
is with my writing. What form will I employ at a given moment?
It depends entirely on how I feel at the time. There's no set rota-
tion, no predetermined sequence—instead, I let things take their
own natural course, following wherever my heart leads. "I want to
start planning a longer work," I may think, or, on another occasion,
"I feel like writing short stories." Once that feeling has made itself
clear, I can select the appropriate container. I never have any problem deciding which one to choose. "This is what I'm doing now,"

I decide, and that's that. If it's short stories I'm writing, I focus on them and ignore everything else.

Still, when all is said and done, I consider myself first and foremost a writer of full-length novels. I approach short stories and novellas with the same focus, and regard the finished works with affection, but my principal battleground has been and remains the novel: some may disagree, but I think it is there that my most distinctive—and probably my best—qualities as a writer stand out. My makeup is that of a long-distance runner, which means I need considerable time and distance to pull things together in a full and comprehensive way. If I were an airplane, I would be the kind that requires a lengthy runway to get off the ground.

Short stories are agile vehicles that can be maneuvered to cover the smaller topics that novels can't handle very well. They are perfect for launching bold new experiments, whether stylistic or plot-based, and treating material for which their form is particularly well suited. They are like a fine net that can scoop up and give shape to hard-to-grasp aspects of my inner self. And they don't require much time to write. If I am in the mood, I can turn one out in a few days in a single spontaneous flow. There are times when I find the short story's lightness and versatility to be an absolute necessity. Nevertheless—and here I must stipulate that I am speaking only *for myself*—the form does not give me the room to express all that is within me in the way I want.

When I set out to write a novel that is likely to possess special meaning to me—in other words, a comprehensive, potentially transformative work—I need free access to a vast, unlimited space. Once I am sure that space exists and that I have stockpiled enough energy to fill it, I open the spigots full blast, so to speak, and settle in for the long haul. Nothing can surpass the fullness I experience then.

It is a special feeling, one I get only when I am launching a long novel.

It strikes me that, at the risk of exaggeration, long novels are my lifeblood, while short stories and novellas are more like practice pieces, important and useful steps toward the construction of longer works. You could compare this to the way long-distance runners think—we may keep track of our records in the five-thousand- and ten-thousand-meter races, but our true standard is our time in the marathon.

So let me now talk about how I compose my novels. More specifically, I would like to speak generally about how I write, using my long novels as concrete examples. Of course, just as the content of my novels differs from one to the next, so do the manner of their composition, where they were written, and how long they took to complete. Nevertheless, as far as I can tell, the overall pattern—the basic sequence of steps, the "rules" I follow and so forth—doesn't vary that much. This formula, if it can be called that, pushes me to establish a fixed routine within my life and work—then and only then does writing a full-length novel become possible. Since a novel is a long-term project requiring an inordinate amount of energy, creating this solid base is absolutely crucial. If I screw that up, my strength may give out partway through.

The first step in my novel-writing process is, metaphorically, to clean off my desk. My stance is that I will work on nothing but the novel until it is completed, so I need to prepare. If I happen to be writing a series of essays, for example, I have to break it off, at least for the time being. Unless something really extraordinary comes along, all new projects are turned down. I'm the sort of person who when I throw myself into one thing, can't do anything else. It's true that I often work on translations while writing a novel, but those are done at my own pace and without any deadline, and I use them to give me a break from my writing. Translation is a technical process, so it uses a different part of the brain than creative writing. Rather than hindering the progress of a novel, therefore, working simultaneously on a translation can actually aid in the process by helping me keep my mental balance, a bit like stretching before exercising.

"This all sounds very fine and dandy," a fellow writer may counter, "but the fact is, we have to take on other sorts of projects to survive. How can we write our novel the way you suggest and still get by financially?" Believe me, I know the problem—what I'm describing here is just the system I myself have developed. It would be great if an author could receive an advance on his work to meet expenses, but Japanese publishers rarely offer advances. I established this system in the early days when my novels weren't selling that well. For some time I held a regular job (manual labor, more or less) to get by. That allowed me to hold on to my basic principle of accepting no commissions while a novel was in process. There were a few exceptions at the very beginning—when my writing style was still a work in progress, and I was proceeding by trial and error—but otherwise I stuck to my guns.

At a certain point in my career, I began to do a good deal of my writing abroad, the reason being that there were just too many trivial distractions in Japan. In a foreign country, I could focus on my work. It seems that for me, living elsewhere is especially helpful in the crucial early stages of a novel, when I am setting up my daily routine, establishing the kind of schedule I need to write. The first time I did this, in the late 1980s, I wasn't at all sure I was making the right choice. Could I really survive under those conditions?

I am a pretty nervy kind of guy, but all the same I felt as if I were heading off to fight a decisive battle, burning bridges behind me as I went. After all, my plan was to live on our savings, and those would eventually give out, even though I had been able to wangle a small advance from my publisher by promising to write a book about my trip (*A Distant Drum*, as it turned out).

In any case, my big decision to explore the possibilities abroad and leave Japan behind turned out to be the right one. Not only did the novel I wrote on this first trip, *Norwegian Wood*, happen to sell well (far better than I expected), providing me with financial security, it also allowed me to establish a system of writing that I have been able to continue ever since. In a sense, I was lucky. But it was more than just luck. At the risk of sounding arrogant, things turned out the way they did because I was so determined, and also prepared to take the consequences.

W HEN WRITING A NOVEL, my rule is to produce roughly ten Japanese manuscript pages (the equivalent of sixteen hundred English words) every day. This works out to about two and a half pages on my computer, but I base my calculations on the old system out of habit. On days where I want to write more, I still stop after ten pages; when I don't feel like writing, I force myself to somehow fulfill my quota. Why do I do it this way? Because it is especially important to maintain a steady pace when tackling a big project. That can't work if you write a lot one day and nothing at all the next. So I punch in, write my ten pages, and then punch out, as if I'm working on a time card.

That's not how an artist should go about his art, some may say. It sounds more like working in a factory. And I concur—that's not how artists work. But why must a novelist be an artist? Who made that rule? No one, right? So why not write in whatever way is most natural to you? Moreover, refusing to think of oneself as an artist removes a lot of pressure. More than being artists, novelists should think of themselves as "free"—"free" meaning that we are able to do what we like, when we like, in a way we like without worrying about how the world sees us. This is far better than wearing the stiff and formal robes of the artist.

Isak Dinesen once said, "I write a little every day, without hope and without despair." I write my ten pages the same way. Cool and detached. "Without hope and without despair" says it perfectly. I wake early each morning, brew a fresh pot of coffee, and work for four or five hours straight. Ten pages a day means three hundred pages a month. That works out to eighteen hundred pages in six months. To give you a concrete sense of how much that is, the first draft of *Kafka on the Shore* was eighteen hundred manuscript pages long. I wrote most of that novel on the North Shore of the Hawaiian island of Kauai. Not only was nothing there to distract me, it rained almost all the time, so the work progressed at a rapid pace. I started the draft in April and wrapped it up in October. I remember the dates particularly well because they coincided perfectly with the baseball season: I began when it did and finished when the Japan Series was just underway. That was the year that the Yakult Swallows, led by their manager Katsuya Nomura, won the Series. As a longtime Swallows fan, I recall how good it felt to tick off those two events together. Swallows' championship done! Novel draft done! My only regret was that, since I was holed up in Kauai writing, I hadn't been able to visit Jingu Stadium to see many of their regular season games in person.

Unlike baseball, however, no sooner has one season (the first draft) ended than a new one begins: that of rewriting. No time is better spent than the time I spend rewriting, and nothing is more fun.

First, though, I take a short break (it depends on the situation, but usually about one week) before undertaking the first rewrite. Then I start at the beginning and plow straight through to the end. At this stage, I make sweeping changes, leaving nothing untouched. No matter how long the novel is, or how complex its structure, I will have composed it without any fixed outline, not knowing how it will unfold or end, letting things take their course and improvising as I go along. This is by far the most fun way to write. As a result, though, the story is riddled with all sorts of contradictions and inconsistencies. Characters may radically change partway through. The timeline may become tangled. These glitches must be fixed if the novel is to flow smoothly in a comprehensible manner. In the process, some lengthy sections may have to be cut back, while other sections may have to be expanded. Entirely new episodes may have to be added.

In the case of *The Wind-Up Bird Chronicle*, I decided that a large chunk of what I had written didn't fit into the whole, so I excised it and used it as the base for a subsequent novel, *South of the Border, West of the Sun*. That's an extreme example, though—in most cases, the sections I cut out are gone forever.

This rewrite usually takes a month or two. When I finish, I break for another week or so and then begin the second rewrite. As with the first rewrite, I start at the head and work my way through. The difference is that now I focus on the details of the manuscript, fine-tuning passages of natural description, for example, and adjusting the tone of the dialogues. I check to ensure that nothing in the plot is out of place, that hard-to-read sections are made easier, and that the story flows smoothly and naturally. No major surgery takes place during this stage, just lots of nips and tucks. Once I have finished, I take another break and then plunge into the third rewrite. This time no cutting is involved. Instead, I tweak the novel, tightening a screw here, loosening a screw there, making sure that all is in place.

Novels are, by definition, longer works, which means the reader can be stifled if the screws are too tight. Correspondingly, there are spots where I leave them loose, to allow the reader room to breathe. There must also be a balance between the novel as a whole and its parts. All these things require careful adjustment. Some critics like to extract one section of text and castigate the writer for its sloppiness, a practice that strikes me as quite unfair. After all, a novel—like a living, breathing human being—needs to have its loose and sloppy parts. Only that way can the tightly constructed sections achieve their full effect.

At this stage of the game, I take a longer break. For two weeks to a month, if possible, I stick the manuscript in my desk drawer and forget it. At least I try to. In the interim I may take a trip, or concentrate on my translating. The time spent working on a long novel is important, to be sure, but time spent doing nothing is no less so. The same principle applies to a factory or a construction site: manufactured goods are left to *settle* before being shipped, and concrete is cured in the open air before being built upon. It is through this process that materials are allowed to set or dry out. The same thing holds true with novels. If you fail to let a novel sit for a certain length of time, the parts won't adhere, or will fail to dry and therefore be weakened.

Once the novel has fully settled, it is time for another detailed and exhaustive run-through. Thanks to my time away, my impressions of the work will have changed quite a lot. Weaknesses I haven't noticed before jump out at me. I can sense what has depth and what doesn't. Just as the work has settled, so too has my state of mind.

Once the settling period is over and the subsequent rewrite completed, I move on to the next step. By this point, the novel has assumed what will be more or less its final form, so I can show it to a first reader—namely, my wife. This is a natural extension of the writing process, a station on the line that leads from inception to completion. My wife's opinions are something like standard tuning in music. They are similar to the old speakers I have at home (sorry, dear!). I have listened to all my records on those speakers. They aren't especially good, part of a JBL system I bought back in the 1970s. Big and bulky, their tonal range is more limited than the fancy new speakers available nowadays. The clarity of the sound isn't as good, either. One could even call them antiques. Yet I have been listening to so many kinds of music on them for so long that they have become my standard of comparison. They are like a part of me.

This may make some people angry, but although literary editors in Japan are specialists, in the end they are company employees who can be reassigned at any time. Of course there are exceptions, but by and large they are appointed by upper management to "look after" you, which means there is no telling how long the relationship may last. For better or for worse, however, my wife is unlikely to be reassigned. She is thus the "fixed point" in my editing process, the one who knows best how I write. We have been together for a long time, so that for the most part I understand the nuances of her thoughts and opinions and where they are coming from. (I have to say "for the most part"—understanding one's wife completely is fundamentally impossible.)

This doesn't mean that I accept her comments easily. After all, I have just finished a novel that took a long time to write, and though the settling process may enable me to look at it more coolly, I am still emotionally wrapped up in the project, so it is very hard for me if someone says anything at all critical about it. I can become quite passionate. Harsh words are sometimes exchanged. I could never be so direct and honest with an editor—that's the advantage, I guess, of getting feedback from someone close to you. I'm a pretty even-tempered guy most of the time, but at this stage in the process I can't help flaring up. I guess it's a necessary outlet, a way for me to release all those pent-up feelings.

There are times when I come to accept her criticisms. "Yeah, she was right about that," I may think, or "Maybe she had something there." It can take a few days to reach that point, though. At other times I find myself disagreeing with her. "No way," I'll decide, after giving it some thought. "This is right as it is." There is a rule that I follow, though, once another person has entered the scene. Whether I agree or disagree with their comments, I rewrite every scene they have found fault with. From start to finish. In those cases where I find myself rejecting their comments, I may take the scene in an entirely different direction.

Whichever course I have followed, once I have sat down and rewritten a given section I almost always find it much improved. It seems that when a reader has a problem, there is usually *something* that needs fixing, whether or not it corresponds to their suggestions. In short, the flow of their reading has been *blocked*. It is my job, then, to eliminate that blockage, to unclog the pipe, as it were.

How to do that is up to me, the author. Even if I feel "That section was perfectly written—there's no need to change anything," I still head back to my desk and work it out. After all, the idea that anything can be "perfectly written" is a clear fallacy.

This time I don't have to go through the manuscript from beginning to end. All I have to do is rewrite those problematic sections. After that, I ask my reader to revisit those parts, we discuss them, and if need be, I work on them some more. Then I show them again to my reader, and if she is still dissatisfied we repeat the whole process. Once we have sorted things out to the best of our capability, I undertake another full rewrite to check and adjust the flow of the work. If fiddling around with small sections has disrupted the tone of the whole, I fix that. Then and only then do I formally present my manuscript to my editor. By this stage of the game my overheated brain has cooled enough to allow me to cope with his comments in an appropriately dispassionate way.

THIS BRINGS UP an interesting story about the creation of the novel *Dance Dance Dance*, which I wrote in the late 1980s. It was the first time I had used a word processor (a Fujitsu laptop) to write. I composed most of the novel in our apartment in Rome, and then finished it off in London, England. When we moved from Rome to London, I stored what I had written on floppy disks, but when I checked after our arrival I discovered one entire chapter was missing. I was a greenhorn when it came to word processors, so it was likely my oversight. Not an uncommon story. Of course it hit me hard. I grew quite depressed. It was a long chapter, and I flattered myself that it had been beautifully written. Not the sort of loss I could dismiss with a wave of my hand.

Still, I couldn't go on sighing and shaking my head forever. So I pulled myself together and tried to resurrect passages that I had sweated over several weeks before. "Did I do it this way?" I wondered. "Or perhaps it was like this." In the end, the resurrection was completed, and the novel was published with the rewritten section. Some time later, however, the part that had gone missing popped up out of nowhere. Somehow it had found its way into a completely different folder. Again, not an uncommon occurrence. What should I do, I worried, if the original turned out to be better than its replacement? When I read it over, however, I was relieved to see that in fact the rewrite was far superior.

What this story shows is that, no matter what you have written, it can be made better. We may feel that what we have turned out is excellent, even perfect, but the fact remains there is always room for improvement. That's why I strive to set aside my pride and self-regard when rewriting, and cool the passions generated by the creative process. I have to be careful not to cool them too much, though, since that would make rewriting impossible. I also have to prepare myself to handle the comments that come from my outside readers. Though their criticisms may hurt, I still must somehow find the patience to listen to what they are saying. By contrast, I don't take criticisms that come out after a novel is published all that seriously. If I worried too much about that stuff, I couldn't go on! When the writing process is still underway, however, I have to be able to incorporate criticisms and suggestions in as humble and open-minded a way as possible. This is and has always been my firm belief.

During my many years as a novelist there have been editors with whom I have not seen eye to eye. They were not bad people, and I'm sure they worked well with other writers, but when it came to editing my books the chemistry just wasn't there. Their opinions often left me shaking my head, and there were times (to be honest) when they really got on my nerves. I could even get angry. Nevertheless, I had to make it work somehow—it was our job, after all.

On one occasion, when we were at the manuscript stage of a novel, I did a rewrite of all the sections the editor had queried. In most cases, however, I rewrote them in a way that was the opposite of what he had suggested: when he instructed "Make this section longer," for example, I made it shorter, and expanded the sections he wanted me to cut down. Pretty outrageous behavior, I know, but the rewrite that resulted turned out to be a big improvement. Thanks to our exchange, the novel was far better than it would have been otherwise. Paradoxically, he turned out to be a very *useful* editor for me. Far more helpful, at least, than those editors who told me only what I wanted to hear. To my way of thinking, at least.

What's crucial, in short, is the *physical act* of rewriting. What carries more weight than anything else is the resolve to sit down at one's desk to improve what one has written. Compared to that, the question of which direction to take in those improvements may be of secondary importance. A writer's instinct and intuition derive less from logic and more from the level of determination brought to the task. It's like beating the bushes to flush out the birds. What difference does it make what kind of stick you use or how you swing it? Neither matters as long as the birds take to the air. It is that flurry of movement that jolts our field of vision, allowing us to see things in a new light. This is my opinion, anyway, crude though it may be.

At any rate, I spend as much time as I can on the rewriting process. I listen to the advice of the people around me (even if it makes me angry) and try to bear it in mind as I rework my novel. Their comments are valuable. Anyone who has just finished writing a long novel is bound to be in an emotional, overstimulated state. In a way, we are out of our minds. This makes sense, since anyone in their right mind would never undertake to write a novel in the first place. Given the circumstances, therefore, it is perfectly acceptable to be deranged as long as you are aware of that fact. For like it is with all crazy people, the opinions of the sane are really important to you.

That does not mean, of course, that you must swallow whole whatever others tell you. Some of their opinions are bound to miss the mark or be entirely wrong. Nevertheless, since they are uttered by those of sound mind, they carry a *certain meaning* for you, *whatever they are.* They will cool you down to a more proper temperature. Such opinions are nothing less than those of the world at large—in short, those who will read your book. If you ignore them, you can bet that they will probably ignore you. Some of you may say, "That's perfectly all right with me." I have no problem with that. If, however, you are a writer who wants to maintain contact with the outside world (and I think most writers do), then it is important to ensure that you have one or two people near you who will read your work, "fixed points" that you can use to orient yourself to your surroundings. Naturally, those fixed points should be able and willing to communicate with you in a frank and honest manner. Even if you flip out every time you hear criticism!

HOW MANY TIMES do I rewrite? There is no specific number. There are countless rewrites at the manuscript stage, and I ask for new galleys many times during the proofreading process, much to my editor's dismay. I mark the galleys up in pencil until each page is covered in black and send them off, then mark them up again when the clean copy is returned. Over and over again. As I said before, writing is a profession that requires stamina, and in truth, I don't mind. The fact is, I have a deep-rooted love for tinkering, so I have no problem reading a passage multiple times to check its rhythm, or fiddling with its word order, or making tiny adjustments to its expression. I like looking at the galleys being covered in black, and the ten or so No. 2 pencils wearing down to stubs on my desk. I don't know why, but I can't get enough of it. I could go on like that forever and not get tired.

Raymond Carver, a writer I love and respect, also enjoyed tinkering. He wrote, about another writer, that "he knew he was finished with a short story when he found himself going through it and taking out commas and then going through the story again and putting commas back in the same places." I know that feeling exactly, for I have had the same experience many times. You reach the limit. If you tinker any more you will only damage what you have written. It's a subtle point, easy to miss. The bit about replacing commas hits it right on the head.

So that's how I go about writing my novels. Some people really like them, and others don't. It takes all kinds. I myself am far from satisfied with things I wrote in the past. I am keenly aware of how much better they could be if I wrote them today. That's why I pick them up only if I absolutely must—they contain so many weaknesses!

All the same, I am sure they were the best that I could do *at that time*. That's because I know the absolute effort that went into them. I spent as much time as I needed and exerted all the strength I had to bring them to completion. It was the equivalent of all-out war. That satisfaction of having given it my all remains with me even now. My novels have never been written on request, so I have not been hounded by deadlines. I have written what I wanted, when I wanted, in the way I wanted. I can state that much with confidence. Seldom have I had to look back and say, "I wish I'd done that differently."

There's another aspect of time one must take into account when writing a novel. That is the "gestation period," something especially important when writing a long work. The "quiet time" spent germinating and cultivating the seeds of what is growing within you. Through this internal process you build up the zeal to tackle the novel. Only the author knows for sure if enough time has been invested in each step of the process: completing the initial preparatory work, giving the ideas concrete shape, letting them fully "settle" in a cool, dark place, exposing them to the natural light when they are ready, carefully inspecting them, and then *tinkering*. The quality of the time spent doing these things will manifest itself in the persuasiveness of the completed work. It is an invisible process, but the difference it makes is huge.

A fitting metaphor for this might be soaking in the tub at home versus doing the same thing in a hot spring. Even if the water in the hot spring is tepid, the heat seeps into your very bones and stays with you long after you get out. A bath at home, by contrast, doesn't penetrate so deeply, and no sooner have you gotten out than you start feeling chilly. I think most Japanese will know what I am talking about. When we enter a hot spring we heave a deep sigh of contentment, for we immediately feel the difference on our skin. If we try to explain that feeling to someone who has never visited a hot spring, we find ourselves at a loss for words.

I think great literature, and great music, follow a somewhat similar pattern. While the temperature of the bathwater at home and at the hot spring may be similar, soaking our naked bodies in them yields different results. We know this through our skin. Yet that "physical" knowledge cannot be expressed in language. The best we can do is "Yeah, the heat seeps in somehow—can't really explain it." If someone counters, "But the temperature is the same—it must be psychological," then we (especially someone as ignorant of science as I am) can offer little in reply.

This is why I am able to shrug off harsh—sometimes unbelievably harsh—criticisms of my work with an "Oh, well, what can you do?" I know at the physical level that I cut no corners in the writing; that I gave it all I had. I spent whatever time was needed to gestate the novel and let it settle, and further time tinkering to get it right. This is why I never feel down or lose my confidence, however much I am criticized. Sure, it bothers me on occasion, but not all that much. I believe that any work into which so much time has been invested will pay off in the end. Time will tell. There are some things in this world whose value will become apparent only after many years have passed. If I weren't certain of that I might grow depressed, however thick my skin. As long as I'm confident that I did everything I should have done, without stinting, there is nothing I need to fear. I can place my future in the hands of time. If we treat time with all the respect, prudence, and courtesy it deserves, it will become our ally.

Raymond Carver wrote the following in a 1982 essay he wrote for *The New York Times,* "A Story-Teller's Shoptalk":

> "It would have been better if I'd taken the time." I was dumbfounded when I heard a novelist friend say this. I still am, if I think about it, which I don't. It's none of my business. But if the writing can't be made as good as it is within us to make it, then why do it? In the end, it's all we have, the only thing we can take into the grave. I wanted to say to my friend, for heaven's sake go do something else. There have to be easier and maybe more honest ways to try and earn a living. Or else just do it to the best of your abilities, your talents, and then don't justify or make excuses. Don't complain, don't explain.

These are harsh words from the usually gentle and genial Carver, but I totally agree with what he is trying to say. I don't know how things are at present, but back in the old days there were quite a few Japanese writers who went around bragging that they couldn't complete a novel unless a deadline was hanging over their heads. This was considered cool in the literati tradition of that era, I guess, but there is a limit to how far that kind of helter-skelter, seat-of-the-pants approach to writing can carry you. You may be able to get away with it when you are young, even turn out some fine work, but it is my impression that a writer's style becomes strangely impoverished if he carries on like that over the long haul.

In my opinion, using your willpower to control time is what makes it your ally. You mustn't let it go on controlling you. That just makes you passive. "Time and tide wait for no man," they say, so if time isn't going to wait for you, you have no choice but to take it to heart and actively construct your schedule on that principle.

In other words, assume command of the situation and stop being passive!

I HAVE NO IDEA if my work is any good, or if it is, to what degree. As the author, it's hardly my place to voice an opinion. Readers have to decide for themselves. As for the value of my books, well, all an author can do is wait quietly for the passing of time to make that clear. At this stage of the game, all I can say is that I gave of myself unsparingly—to quote Carver again, my works are "as good as it is within me to make them." Since I put everything into their creation, I will never have to say, "It would have been better if I'd taken the time." Whatever limitations they have are the result of my own deficiencies at the stage I wrote them, nothing more. That's too bad, but nothing for me to be ashamed of. Deficiencies can be overcome if you work hard enough. A missed opportunity, however, can never be regained.

Over the years, I have taken pains to maintain and preserve the system that has made this approach to writing possible, making sure to keep it well oiled and free of dirt or rust. In my own small way, I feel proud to have sustained it to this point. In fact, I think I enjoy talking about my system much more than I do talking about the value and specific qualities of the various books I have written. I think this kind of talk has more *practical* value as well.

If readers experience even a little of the warmth from a hot-spring bath when reading my works, then I am truly happy. I myself seek such warmth in the books I read and the music I listen to.

Forget all the chatter—we should trust in our felt experience above all else. For the author, and for his readers, that alone is the ultimate standard.

A Completely Personal
and Physical Occupation

↳

WRITING FICTION is an entirely personal process that takes place in a closed room. Shut away in a study, you sit at a desk and (in most cases) create an imaginary story out of nothing and put it in the form of writing. The formless and subjective is transformed into something tangible and objective (or at least something that seeks to be objective). Defined simply, this is the day-to-day work we novelists perform.

I'm sure there are many people who will say, "But wait, I don't have anything like a study." The same was true for me when I started out writing—I had nothing resembling a study to work in. In my tiny apartment near the Hatonomori Hachiman Shrine in Sendagaya (in a building that's since been torn down) I sat at the kitchen table late at night after my wife had gone to bed, scratching away with a pen on Japanese-style manuscript paper. That's how I wrote my first two novels, *Hear the Wind Sing* and *Pinball, 1973*. "Kitchen-table" fiction is what I've dubbed these early works.

When I first started writing *Norwegian Wood*, I wrote at cafés in various places in Greece, on board ferry boats, in the waiting lobbies of airports, in shady spots in parks, and at desks in cheap hotels. Hauling around oversized, four-hundred-character-per-page Japanese manuscript paper was too much, so in Rome I bought a cheap notebook (the kind we used to call college-ruled notebooks) and wrote the novel down in tiny writing with a disposable Bic pen. I still had to contend with noisy cafés, wobbly tables that made writing difficult, coffee spilling on the pages, and at night in my hotel room when I'd go over what I'd written, sometimes there would be couples getting all hot and heavy beyond the paper-thin walls separating my room from the room next door. Things weren't easy, in other words. I can smile at these memories now, but at the time it was all pretty discouraging. I had trouble finding a decent place to live, and moved all over Europe, all the while continuing to work on my novel. And I still have that thick old notebook, with its coffee stains (or whatever they are; I'm not really sure about some of them).

Wherever a person is when he writes a novel, it's a closed room, a portable study. That's what I'm trying to say.

Essentially, I believe people don't write novels because someone asks them to. They write because they have a personal *desire to write*. And it's this strong inner motivation that drives them to write, and to endure all their own struggles as they do.

Naturally, some writers write novels because they've been asked to do so. This might be true for the majority of professional writers. My own personal policy for many years has been not to write novels because I've been contracted to or requested to, but I might be a rare case. For most writers, editors will ask them to write a short story, for instance, for their company's magazine, or a novel exclusively for their publishing company, and they'll go from there. In these cases it's usual to have a deadline, and depending on the situation, to receive a payment up front as a kind of advance.

But the fact remains that novels are written on the novelist's own initiative, out of an inner motivation. Perhaps there are people who can't get started writing without those conditions—a specific request from a publisher and a deadline. But even so, deadlines and piles of money and pleas from publishers still aren't enough to get someone to write a novel unless he's motivated from inside to write. I think that goes without saying.

But no matter what triggers the writing, once a novelist sits down to write a novel he's utterly alone with the task. No one is there to help him (or her). Some novelists might have help from researchers, but all they do is gather materials helpful to the novelists. No one else orders all those materials in his or her mind, and no one else finds the right words for him to use. Once you begin, you have to forge ahead by yourself, and complete the novel on your own. It's not like baseball these days, where if a pitcher can get through seven innings he can then hand things over to a relief pitcher and take a break on the bench. For a novelist there's no bullpen, and no relief pitchers in sight. So even if the game goes into extra innings—fifteen innings, even eighteen—you have to keep on pitching until it's decided.

For example—and this is based on my own case—writing a novel means sitting alone in my study for over a year (sometimes two or even three years), diligently writing away. I get up early and focus solely on writing for five to six hours every single day. Thinking that hard and long about things, your brain gets overheated (with my scalp literally getting hot at times), so after that I need to give my head a rest. That's why I spend my afternoons napping, enjoying music, reading innocuous books. That kind of life, though, gets you out of shape physically, so every day I spend about an hour outdoors exercising. That sets me up for the next day's work. Day after day, without exception, I repeat this cycle.

It's kind of a cliché to say it's a lonely process, but writing a novel—especially a really long one—is exactly that: extremely lonely work. Sometimes I feel like I'm sitting all alone at the bottom of a well. Nobody will help me, and nobody's there to pat me on the back and tell me I've done a great job. The novel I produce may be praised by people (if it turns out well), but no one seems to appreciate the process itself that led to it. That's a burden the writer must carry alone.

I'm a very patient type of person, I think, when it comes to that kind of process. Still, at times I do get fed up with it and hate it. But as I work away, persevering day after day—like a bricklayer carefully laying one brick on top of another—I reach a certain point where I get the definite feeling that when all is said and done, a writer is exactly what I am. And I accept that feeling as something good, something to be celebrated. The slogan of AA (Alcoholics Anonymous) in the US is "One day at a time," and that's exactly what this is like. Maintaining a set rhythm, steadily hauling in one day after the other and sending them on their way. Silently continue to do this and at a certain point *something* happens inside you. But it takes time to reach this point. And until then you have to be very patient. One day is just one day. You can't take care of two or three days' worth all at once.

What do you need in order to patiently keep on going?

Needless to say, it's stamina.

If you can only manage to sit at your desk and focus for three days, you'll never be a novelist. I'm sure someone will say if you can do that for three days you should be able to write a short story. True enough. If you work three days you might be able to manage *one* short story. But completing a short story over three days, then going back to square one, and getting yourself up for another three days to write the next short story, is not a cycle anyone could keep up for long. If a writer tried to maintain that kind of compartmentalized process for long, I think his health would fail. Even those who specialize in short stories have to have a certain continuity in their life as professional writers. Whether you write novels or short stories, to maintain creativity over a long period of time you need the kind of staying power that makes this continual process possible.

Well, then, what do you need to do to acquire that kind of stamina?

I HAVE BUT ONE ANSWER, and a very simple one: you have to become physically fit. You need to become robust and physically strong. And make your body your ally.

This is all my own personal opinion, of course, based on my own experience. There might not be any universal application. But I'm speaking here as one individual to begin with, so my opinions are, no matter what, individual and experiential. I'm sure there are differing opinions, but you need to hear those from other people. I'm only giving my own personal opinions here. It's up to you to decide if there's anything universally applicable about them.

Most people think that since the work of a novelist just involves sitting at a desk and writing, it has nothing to do with physical stamina. They seem to think that as long as you have enough strength in your fingers to tap away at a computer keyboard (or write on paper with a pen) that's all you need. There's still a deep-rooted sense that writers are, in the first place, unhealthy, antisocial, and unconventional, so maintaining good health or physical fitness is beside the point. And to some extent I can understand that objection. Such a stereotypical image of writers is not easily overcome.

However, if you try writing yourself, you'll no doubt understand that sitting at a desk in front of a computer screen (or even at an empty orange crate with manuscript paper on top, there's no difference) every day for five or six hours, focused solely on creating a story, requires an extraordinary amount of physical strength. When you're young this might not be so hard. In your twenties and thirties you're brimming with vitality and your body doesn't complain when it's overworked. Focus and concentration, too, are relatively easy to summon up when needed, and can be maintained at a high level. It's truly wonderful to be young. (Not that if I were told to relive my youth I'm sure I'd want to.) But generally speaking, once you reach middle age, unfortunately, physical strength declines, dynamic strength deteriorates, and you lose stamina. Your muscles atrophy, and you put on unneeded pounds. As far as our bodies go, the bitter truth is that it's easy to lose muscles and easy to put on weight. And to make up for that decline, sustained, self-directed effort is needed to maintain one's physical strength.

And as physical strength declines (I'm speaking in general terms here), there is a subtle decline in mental fitness, too. Mental agility and emotional flexibility are lost. Once when I was interviewed by a young writer I declared that "once a writer puts on fat, it's all over." This was a bit hyperbolic, and of course there are exceptions, but I do believe that for the most part it's true. Whether it is actual physical fat or metaphoric fat. Most writers are able to compensate for this through improved writing technique or a more mature consciousness, but there is a limit to these as well.

Recent research shows that aerobic exercise leads to a rapid increase in the number of neurons produced in the hippocampus in the brain. Aerobic exercise is sustained exercise such as swimming or jogging. However, if left as is, in twenty-eight hours these newly formed neurons will disappear without having served any purpose. It's a real waste. But give these newly formed neurons some intellectual stimulation and they are activated—they connect with the network in the brain and become an organic part of the signal-transfer community. In other words, the network within the brain becomes broader and denser. The ability to learn and remember is elevated. And this makes it easier for our minds to respond to changed circumstances and for us to display exceptional creativity. We can think in more complex ways and can come up with bolder, original ideas. In other words, the everyday combination of physical exercise and the intellectual process provides an ideal influence on the type of creative work the writer is engaged in.

I began running once I became a full-time writer (I started when I was writing *A Wild Sheep Chase*), and for thirty years running for an hour a day, or sometimes swimming, has been a regular part of my daily schedule. Perhaps I have an inherently strong constitution, but during this time I've never been seriously ill and never hurt my legs or back (though I did sustain a torn muscle once when playing squash), and I have continued to run every day with hardly ever taking a break. Once a year I run a full marathon, and I've participated in triathlons as well.

People tell me I must have a strong will, running like that every day, but the way I see it, it's much more physically trying for ordinary company employees who ride in crowded commuter trains every day. Compared to riding for an hour in a rush-hour train, running for an hour outside whenever you feel like it is nothing. It's not that I have a particularly strong will. I enjoy running and am just continuing something that suits my personality. No matter how strong your will might be, you're not going to do something for thirty years if it doesn't suit you.

And as I've followed this lifestyle, I get the feeling every day that my ability as a writer is gradually improving, and my creativity is becoming more secure and steady. Not that I can demonstrate this convincingly, with objective facts and figures, but I do have a strong, indelible sense inside me that this is what is happening.

But whenever I explained this to people, most of them never listened. In fact, most tended to scoff. Especially until about ten years ago, most people didn't get it at all. Most people said something like "If you run every day like that, you'll get too healthy and won't be able to write anything worthwhile." To make matters worse, in the literary world there was a tendency to flatly feel contempt for any physical discipline or training. Mention "health maintenance" and many people imagine some muscle-bound macho types; but regular aerobic exercise done to keep healthy and bodybuilding done using all kinds of equipment are two very different things.

For a long time I myself wasn't exactly sure what it meant to me to run every day. If you run every day, then of course it'll make you healthy. You lose fat and are able to have well-balanced muscles, and can control your weight. But as I run, I feel *that's not all there is to it*. There's *something more important* deeper down in running. But it's not at all clear to me what that something is, and if I don't understand it myself, then I can't explain it to others.

Still, not grasping what it all means, I persist in my daily running routine. Thirty years is a long time. To continue one habit that long requires a great deal of effort. How have I been able to do it? It's because I feel like the act of running represents, concretely and succinctly, some of the *things I have to do in this life*. I have that sort of general, yet very strong, sense. So even on days when I think I'm not feeling so great and don't feel like running, I tell myself, "No matter what, this is something I have to do in my life," and I go out and run without really ascribing a logical reason for it. That sentence has become a kind of mantra for me: *No matter what, this is something I have to do in my life.*

It's not that I think *running is a great thing*. Running is just running. There's no good or bad about it. If you think "I hate running," then there's no need for you to run. It's up to each person whether they run or don't run. I'm not advocating anything like "Hey, everybody, let's all get out there and run!" On winter days when I pass groups of high-school students out on a mandatory morning run, I even feel sympathy for them, feeling, "Those poor kids, there have to be some of them who don't want to be out running." I really do.

For me as an individual, however, the act of running has its own significance. What I mean is, for me, and for the things I'm trying to accomplish in life, I've always had the sort of natural recognition inside that in some form or another it's a necessary act. And it's this feeling that always urges me on. This feeling is what encourages me to *get out there and run today*, even on freezing mornings and blazingly hot afternoons, even when my body feels dull and unwilling.

When I read those science articles about the structure of neurons, it convinced me all over again, that what I've been doing up till now, and the sensations I've had have been on the mark. What I mean is, I felt very strongly that paying close attention to what the body is feeling is, fundamentally, a critical process for someone involved in creative work. Whether it's the emotions or the brain, they're all equally part of our physical body. I don't know what physiologists say about this, but to me, the lines separating the emotional, the mental, and the physical aren't all that clearly defined.

I SAY THIS all the time, so some of you might think "What? That again?"; but it's important, so I'd like to repeat it here. I'm sorry if it comes off sounding overly insistent.

Novelists basically tell stories. And telling stories, to put it another way, means delving deep down into your unconscious. To descend to the darkest realms of the mind. The broader the scale of the story, the deeper the novelist has to descend. It's like constructing a large building, where you need to dig down very deep for the foundation. And the more hidden the story you're telling, the heavier and thicker is that subterranean darkness.

From the midst of that subterranean darkness the novelist finds what he needs—the nourishment needed for the novel, in other words—and returns with it to the upper regions of consciousness. And there he transforms it into the writing, giving it form and meaning. Sometimes that darkness is filled with danger. What exists there often takes on all sorts of forms in order to deceive people. There are no signposts, no maps. Some places are veritable mazes. It's like an underground cave. If you don't keep your wits about you, you'll get lost, maybe unable ever to return to the surface. That darkness contains a mix of the collective unconscious and the individual unconscious, the ancient and the modern. We bring those back with us, without classifying them as one or the other, and sometimes that package can have disastrous results.

What's needed above all to stand up to that deep darkness, and confront daily the various dangers inherent there, is physical strength. I can't give figures to express what level is needed, but the point is, it's far preferable to be strong than not to be. And this strength I'm talking about is not the kind you need to compare with others, but is more the *exact amount of strength* you yourself need. As I've written novels every day, I've slowly come to feel this and understand this. Your mind has to be as tough as possible, and in order to maintain that mental toughness over the long term, it's essential to increase and sustain the receptacle that is physical strength.

This *mental toughness* I'm talking about isn't actual toughness on the level of daily life. In real life I'm just an ordinary person. I get hurt over trivial things and, conversely, shoot my mouth off when I shouldn't and afterwards deeply regret it. I find it hard to resist temptation, and try my best to shirk obligations I have no interest in. I get upset over all kinds of trivial things, then let down my guard and completely overlook things that are really important. I make it a point not to make excuses, yet at times I let them slip out. One day I think I'll skip drinking, then go ahead and grab a beer from the fridge. I imagine this makes me pretty much in line with most people in the world. Or perhaps even below average.

Still, when it comes to writing novels, I'm able to maintain the mental toughness needed to sit at a desk for five hours each and every day. This mental toughness—or at least the greater part of it—isn't something I was born with; it was acquired. I obtained this by consciously training myself. Take it a step further and I would say that, though it isn't *easy* per se, anyone, as long as they make the effort, can achieve this to a certain extent. Naturally, just like physical strength, this isn't something you need to compare to others or use to compete with them, but is the strength you need to maintain the way you yourself are now in the very best condition.

I'm not advocating becoming moralistic or stoic. There's no particular direct relationship between becoming moralistic or stoic and being a great novelist. At least I don't believe there probably is. All I'm doing is advocating something quite simple, and practical: namely, that it's best to become more conscious of the physical side of things.

That way of thinking and living is at odds, perhaps, with the usual image people have of novelists. I'm gripped myself by a growing sense of anxiety as I say this—the sense that many people still expect novelists to conform to the classic image of people who lead a debauched life, ignore their family, pawn their wife's kimono for money (perhaps an image that's a bit out of date), get hooked on alcohol, or women, doing whatever pleases them—the antiestablishment writer who creates literature out of ruin and chaos. Or if not that, then the expectation that the writer be a *man of action*, the kind who takes part in the Spanish Civil War, pounding away at his typewriter as the shells whiz around him. I have the sense that no one is hoping that a writer lives in a quiet suburb, lives a healthy early-to-bed-early-to-rise lifestyle, goes jogging without fail every day, likes to make healthful vegetable salads, and holes up in his study for a set period every day to work. I have the anxious sense that all I'm doing is throwing a damper on people's sense of the romantic.

Consider the case of Anthony Trollope. A novelist in nineteenth-century England, Trollope wrote many lengthy works and was quite popular at the time. He worked at the London post office and started writing novels mainly as a hobby, but then became success-ful as a writer, until he became a leading novelist of his day. Still, he kept his job at the post office. Every morning before work he got up early and wrote a fixed number of pages, and then would set off for work. Trollope was apparently an outstanding civil servant and achieved a high position in the British postal service. It's said that the red mailboxes you see all over London are a legacy of his work in the postal service. (Up until then there were no such things as mailboxes.) He was unusually fond of his work at the post office, and no matter how busy he became as a writer he never considered quitting his day job. I imagine he was a bit of an eccentric.

He passed away in 1882 at the age of sixty-seven, and a posthu-mous autobiography was published that revealed for the first time how unromantic and exceedingly orderly his daily routine was. Up until then people didn't know what sort of person Trollope was, but once the details of his life became known, critics and readers alike were aghast and discouraged, and his popularity and critical reputation as a novelist in England took a decided nosedive. For me, when I heard this story I thought, "Wow, what an amazing guy," and was simply impressed, and respected Trollope all the more (I'll admit to not having read any of his work, though); but his contemporaries reacted the totally opposite way. They were seri-ously upset that they'd been reading novels written by such a *thor-oughly boring* man. Maybe ordinary people in nineteenth-century

England had an idealized image of a novelist, or a novelist's life-style, as unconventional. I get a little jumpy sometimes wondering if I'll suffer the same fate as Trollope, seeing as how I also live this kind of *ordinary* life. Well, it's a good thing, I guess, that in the twentieth century Trollope's critical reputation has seen something of a reassessment . . .

Along the same lines, Franz Kafka wrote his works in the time between working at his job as a civil servant in an insurance company in Prague. He was by all accounts a very able, earnest official, and his colleagues all acknowledged how very capable he was. It was said that if he took a day off work, the company basically ground to a halt. Like Trollope, he never slacked off on his main job, and also was quite serious about writing (I get the sense, though, that he may have used the fact of having a full-time job as an excuse that kept the majority of his works incomplete); but Kafka's case was different from Trollope's in that his regular lifestyle was praised rather than disparaged. Where the difference lies is hard to say. Certainly there's no accounting for people's opinions sometimes.

At any rate, my apologies to all those, as far as novelists go, who are looking for an idealized image of the unconventional—and as I've said over and over, I'm only saying this as it applies to *me*—but practicing physical moderation is indispensable in order to *keep on* being a novelist.

I think chaos exists in everyone's minds. Chaos is in my mind, and in yours as well. It's not the sort of thing, though, that in daily life needs to be given form and openly shown to others. Not something you brag about, saying, "Hey, get a load of how huge the chaos is inside me," or anything. If you want to come face-to-face with the chaos inside you, then be silent and descend, alone, to the depths of your consciousness. The chaos we need to face, the real chaos that's worth coming face-to-face with, is found precisely there. It's hiding right there, at your very feet.

And what you need to faithfully, sincerely verbalize this is a quiet ability to focus, a staying power that doesn't get discouraged, and a consciousness that is, up to a point, firm and systematic. And what you need to consistently maintain these qualities is physical strength. This might be seen as a boring, literally prosaic conclusion, but that's my fundamental way of thinking as a novelist. Whether I'm criticized, praised, have rotten tomatoes thrown at me, or beautiful flowers tossed my way, that's the only way I know how to write—and to live.

I LOVE THE ACTIVITY of writing novels. Which is why I'm really grateful to be able to make a living doing just that, why I feel it's a blessing I've been able to live this kind of life. At a certain point in my life, if I hadn't had an exceptional stroke of good fortune, I never would have been able to achieve this. I honestly feel this way. You might label it a miracle more than good fortune.

Even if I had some inborn talent for writing novels, it would have remained there, like with oil fields or mines, if I hadn't unearthed it: undisturbed, deep underground. Some people insist that if you're truly talented at something, your talent will definitely blossom someday. But based on my own gut feelings—and I trust my gut—that won't necessarily happen. If that talent lies buried in a relatively shallow place, it's very possible it will emerge on its own. But if it's buried deep down, you can't discover it that easily. It can be the most abundant talent, but as long as there's no one to actually pick up a shovel, say "Let's dig here," and start digging, it may remain forever unknown, buried in the earth. When I look back on my own life, I really feel this is true. There's a right time for things, and if you miss that opportunity, most of the time you'll never get a second chance. Life is often capricious, unfair, and sometimes cruel. I was able, by chance, to grab a golden opportunity. Thinking back on it now, I feel it was nothing less than a stroke of good fortune.

But good luck is, so to speak, simply an admission ticket. In that sense it's different from an oil field or a mine. Just getting that admission ticket is no guarantee that everything will be okay after that, that you can then live a life of ease and luxury. The admission ticket allows you into the performance—but that's all. You hand over your admission ticket at the entrance, enter the site, but then what you do there, what you discover, what you gain, what you lose, how you overcome the many obstacles that crop up there, is all a question of individual talent, gifts, and competence, of the person's abilities and outlook. And sometimes it's simply a matter of physical strength. At any rate, you can't make do with just good fortune.

As you might expect, just like there are all kinds of people there are all kinds of novelists. All kinds of lifestyles and ways of writing. Different viewpoints and styles of writing. So they can't all be covered in one blanket statement. All I'm able to do is talk about the type of writer *I* am, so of course you need to qualify what I'm saying. At the same time, though—as far as being a professional writer is concerned—there should be something that goes beyond individual difference and connects us at a fundamental level. In a word, I think this is mental *toughness*. I'm talking about a firm, strong will that allows you to keep on writing novels despite all sorts of difficulties you encounter along the way—the confusion you go through, severe criticism, betrayal by good friends, unexpected failures, the occasional loss of confidence, or overconfidence that makes you slip up.

And if you want to sustain that willpower over the long haul, then your quality of life becomes an issue. First of all, you need to live to the full. And my basic idea is that "living fully" means, to some extent, building up the *framework* that contains the soul, the physical body, and pushing it forward it step by step. Living is (in most cases) a tiresome, lackadaisical, protracted battle. If you don't make the effort to persist in pushing the body forward, then keeping a firm, positive hold over your will and soul becomes, in my opinion, realistically next to impossible. Life isn't that easy. If you tilt toward one direction or the other, sooner or later the opposite side will have its revenge. The scales tilting toward one side will inescapably return to where they were. Physical strength and spiritual strength are like the two pairs of wheels of a car. When they're in balance and are functioning well, then the car operates most efficiently and moves in the optimal direction.

To give a simple example, if you have a cavity and your tooth is aching, you can't sit down and take your time working on a novel. No matter what sort of amazing plot you have in mind, or strong desire to write the novel, and no matter how much talent you might possess to spin out a rich, beautiful story, if you're hit by a constant, sharp physical pain, there's no way you can concentrate on writing. First you have to go to the dentist and get your tooth taken care of— get your body ready to go, in other words—and only then can you sit down to write. Put simply, that's what I'm trying to say.

It's a very simple theory, but it's something I've learned personally through experience. You have to manage physical strength and spiritual strength so they're in balance, so they effectively reinforce each other. The more protracted the fight, the more significance this theory takes on.

Naturally, if you're a rare genius and think that, like Mozart or Schubert, Pushkin or Rimbaud or van Gogh, it's okay to bloom beautifully for a very short time and produce beautiful, sublime works that move people's hearts, make a lasting name for yourself in history, and then burn out, then my theory doesn't apply. Go ahead and totally forget everything I've said up till now. And just do what you want to do, however you want to do it. It goes without saying that that is an admirable way of living. And genius artists like Mozart, Schubert, Pushkin, Rimbaud, and van Gogh are indispensable, in any age.

If you're not like them, however, if you're not (sad to say) a rare genius, and you wish to, gradually, over time, raise the level of the (more or less limited) talent you do have, and make it into something powerful, I believe my theory might be of some value. You toughen up your will as much as you can. And at the same time you equip and maintain the headquarters of that will, your body, to be as healthy as possible, as sturdy as possible, so it doesn't, as much as possible, hinder you—and this will link up with an overall balanced, enhanced quality of your life. My basic idea is that as long as you don't mind putting in honest effort, the quality of the work you produce will also naturally be improved. (To repeat, this theory does not apply to genius artists.)

So, what should you do to raise the quality of your life? The method will be different for each person. Take a hundred people and you'll have a hundred methods. Each person has to discover their own path. Just like each person must discover their own story, and their own style.

To give an example from Franz Kafka again, he died at the young age of forty from tuberculosis, and from the works he left behind, you get the image of a nervous, physically weak person. The truth is, though, he was surprisingly diligent about taking care of himself physically. He was a strict vegetarian, swam a mile in the Moldau River every day in the summer, and exercised daily. Kafka, with an earnest look on his face, exercising—that would have been quite a sight.

As I've lived and matured, I've found, through much trial and error, the way that works best for me. Trollope found the way that works best for him, and so did Kafka. You should find what works best for you. Physically and mentally, everyone's circumstances are different. Everybody has their own theories. However, if my way of doing things might be a useful reference—meaning, that is, if it does have some universality—naturally, that would please me no end.

Regarding Schools

↳

N THIS CHAPTER I'd like to talk about schools. What kind of place (or environment) did I learn from? How did school education help—or not help—me as a novelist? These are the kind of topics I'd like to discuss here.

My parents were both teachers, and I've taught a number of courses myself in universities in the US (though I don't have any special qualifications to do so). But honestly, I never liked school. When I think back on the schools I attended, it pains me to say it (my apologies), but the truth is, they don't call up many pleasant memories. In fact, thinking about them makes my neck throb and ache. Maybe, though, the problem was less with the schools themselves than with me.

At any rate, when at long last I finally graduated from university,

I remember being relieved, thinking, "Great. Now I never have to go to school again." It was like a weight had been lifted from my shoulders. I've never felt any nostalgia about school, not even once (probably).

Okay, then why am I taking the trouble to discuss schools now?

I think it's because I've reached a point—as a person far removed from school now—where it's probably a good idea for me to gather my thoughts and feelings about my own school experience, and about education overall. Or, rather, I get the sense it's an area I need to clarify a bit as I talk about myself. Additionally, another motivation may be conversations I've had recently with a few young people who are part of the trend in Japan of students refusing to attend (or avoiding going to) school.

HONESTLY, from elementary school through college I was never that good a student. Not that I had bad grades or I was a dropout or anything—I managed to get by okay—but the act of studying itself was something I basically disliked, and I really didn't study much. The high school I attended in Kobe was a so-called public college preparatory school, a large school with over six hundred students in each grade. We were part of the baby-boomer generation, so there were tons of kids. They would post the names of the top fifty students in the periodic exams we took in each subject (at least that's my recollection of it), but my name was never on any of the lists. Meaning I was never in that top ten percent of students with excellent grades. If anything, I was probably in the upper middle range.

The reason I didn't study hard was simple. It was boring. I just wasn't interested. There were so many other things in life more fun than studying for school. Reading books, listening to music, going to movies, swimming in the sea, playing baseball, playing around with cats, and when I got a bit older, staying up all night playing mah-jongg with my friends and going on dates with girls . . . Compared to all those, studying for school was a total bore. I guess that goes without saying.

Not that I felt like I was sloughing off studying just to have a good time. Because deep down, I knew that reading lots of books, listening intently to music—and maybe I should include going out with girls, too—was, for me, a personal form of study that had real significance, a significance greater than studying for any tests for school. I can't recall now to what extent I was explicitly aware of this or could have articulated it, but I was aware of being sort of defiantly anti-schoolwork. Of course, if the schoolwork involved a topic that interested me, I'd study it on my own initiative.

Another thing I've never been much interested in is competing with others for ranking. I'm not saying this to make myself look good or anything, but frankly I just couldn't be bothered to care about specific numbers—grades or rank or deviation values (thankfully, when I was a teenager we didn't have that way of ranking students)—used to show where people stood academically. It's just my personality. I do sort of have a tendency to hate to lose (depending on the circumstances), but that doesn't extend much to the level of competing with others.

Anyway, back then, for me reading was more important than anything else. It goes without saying, but there are tons of books that are much more exciting than any textbook. As I turned the pages of those books, I had a vivid, physical sensation, as if the content was becoming part of my flesh and blood. That's why I couldn't buckle down to study for exams. I couldn't see how mechanically cramming information into my head—historical dates, English vocabulary words, and the like—was going to be of any use in the future. Technical knowledge that's memorized mechanically, not systematically, will, over time, scatter away, to be sucked in somewhere and vanish—maybe into some dark graveyard of useless knowledge. Because there's no need to retain it in your memory.

Compared to that, things that stay with you over time are far more important. Obviously. The thing is, though, that sort of knowledge isn't immediately useful. It takes a long time for it to show its true value. That kind of knowledge doesn't directly link up to grades on exams. The difference between immediate value and nonimmediate value is like the difference between a small teakettle and a large one. The small kettle is handy because it boils quickly, but it cools down quickly, too. A large kettle, on the other hand, takes time for the water to boil, but once it does it doesn't cool down for a long time. It's not a question of which one is superior, since each one has its uses and distinctive characteristics. What's important is knowing how to use these differences to your advantage.

FROM ABOUT THE MIDDLE of my time in high school, I started reading English books in the original. My English wasn't great, but I wanted to read the novels in the original, or books that hadn't yet been translated into Japanese, so I bought a pile of English paperbacks from a used-book store down near Kobe harbor, the kind that basically sells them by the pound, and tore through them from cover to cover, whether I understood the meaning completely or not. At first it was more out of curiosity, but then reading in English started to feel more *familiar*, I suppose, and I could read through books in English pretty smoothly. There were a lot of foreigners living in Kobe then, and since it was a port city, there were always many sailors around, and the used-book stores had plenty of English books the sailors had sold to them. Most of the books I read then were mysteries or science fiction, the kind with gaudy covers, and the English wasn't all that difficult. You wouldn't expect a high-school student to be able to sink his teeth into the kind of complex prose of a James Joyce or a Henry James. At any rate, after a while I was able to read an entire book, from start to finish, in English. Curiosity is everything. Not that this led to improved grades in English exams at school—it didn't at all. As always, my grades in English class remained pretty unspectacular.

Why is that? At the time I thought about it long and hard. There were lots of kids who had better grades on English tests than me, but as far as I could tell, none of them could read a book in English from cover to cover. Yet I could easily plow through an entire book. Then why were my grades in English class so mediocre? The conclusion I came to was that the goal of English classes in Japanese high schools was not to get students to use actual, living English.

Then what *was* the goal? There was only one: for students to get high marks on the English section of the college entrance exams. At least for the teachers in the public high school I attended, being able to read books in English or have ordinary conversations with foreigners was beside the point (I won't go so far as to say superfluous). For them it was far more important for us to memorize as many English vocabulary words as we could, master the past perfect subjunctive, and learn to choose the correct prepositions and articles.

That kind of knowledge is, of course, important to have. Especially after I began professionally translating books, I've felt how tenuous my grasp is of that basic grammatical knowledge. But if you feel like it, you can always learn detailed technical knowledge later on. Learn it on an as-needed basis as you work. What's more important is a clear sense of purpose as to why you are studying English (or any other foreign language). If that sense of purpose is vague, then the whole thing becomes pure drudgery. In my case, the goal was crystal clear. I simply wanted to read novels in English, in the original. That's all it was.

Language is a living thing, as are human beings. When living people try to acquire a living language, flexibility is a must. Each side is in motion, and you have to find the most effective point of contact. This may seem obvious, but within the school system it wasn't obvious at all. And I found this really unfortunate. In other words, the school system and the system that was *me* didn't mesh well. As a result, I didn't enjoy going to school. Though having a few good friends, and some cute girls, in the class did keep me going every day.

Of course I'm talking about back in *my day*. I think the situation has changed a lot since then. The world's become much more globalized, the use of technology in schools has improved, and things have gotten much more convenient. But I can't help feeling that the way schools operate, their basic approach, isn't all that different from what it was fifty-some-odd years ago. When it comes to foreign languages, if you really want to learn a living foreign language, the only way is to go abroad. If you go to Europe, you'll find most young people speak pretty fluent English, and they read a lot of books in English as well (which leads publishers of books translated into their various countries' languages to lament the fact that sales aren't so good). But most young Japanese are still not good at handling English outside of school—whether it be speaking, reading, or writing. And this is a major problem. If you leave this kind of distorted educational system in place, I don't think even including English study starting at the elementary-school level, a fairly recent move in Japan, will help much. All it does is increase profits in the education industry.

This goes beyond English, or the study of foreign languages. I can't help thinking that in almost every subject, Japan's educational system fundamentally fails to consider how to motivate each individual to improve their potential. Even now the system seems intent on going by the book to cram in facts and teach test-taking techniques. And teachers and parents live and die by how many of their students and children get into various universities. It's all kind of sad.

When I was in school my parents and teachers always warned me, "You've got to study as hard as you can while you're in school. Otherwise when you grow up you'll regret not having studied more when you were young." But after I left school I never thought that, not even once. For me it was more regret that I hadn't done more things I enjoyed doing. Being forced to do that kind of rote memorization, I felt, wasted my life. But maybe I'm an extreme case.

I'M THE TYPE OF PERSON who whenever I like something and am interested in it, puts everything I have into it and goes all in. I never stop halfway, thinking, "That's good enough." I do it until I'm convinced I've got it. But unless something really grabs me, I can't put my heart into it. Or, more precisely, I just can't work up the desire to do so. I've always been that way, clearly washing my hands of things that didn't hold my interest. If somebody orders me to do something (especially somebody above me), I'll do a perfunctory job at best.

It's the same with sports. From elementary school all the way to college I couldn't stand PE class. Having to put on a gym uniform, march out to the school grounds, and run through exercises was a royal pain. So for a long time I thought I wasn't very athletic. But once I got out into the world and started doing sports that I wanted to do, I loved it. Finding that sports could be so much fun was a great discovery, a real eye opener. Then what was up with the sports I was forced to do at school? The whole thing left me stupefied. No two people are alike, of course, and you can't easily generalize, but to exaggerate at bit, I get the feeling that PE classes exist precisely in order to make people hate sports.

If you divide people into dog types and cat types, I am most definitely the latter. Order me to go right and you can count on me going left. Sometimes I'll feel bad about it, but that's just the way I am. And it's good to have all kinds of personalities in the world. But in my view, the goal of the Japanese educational system appears to be to create doglike people who will be of use to the community . . . and even sometimes to create sheeplike people they can lead as a group to a common destination.

This tendency doesn't just stop with education, but extends to companies and the bureaucracy-centered Japanese social system. That inflexible emphasis on numerical values and the orientation toward the immediate efficacy of rote memorization and the utilitarian produces some terribly harmful effects in all sorts of fields. During a certain period of time, it's true that that utilitarian system functioned well. In the earlier postwar full-steam-ahead period, when the aims and goals of the whole society were generally clear, that approach may have been appropriate. But once postwar reconstruction was over and the period of high economic growth was a thing of the past, after the bubble economy burst, that kind of

"Draw up the fleet and let's all speed toward our destination" type of social system no longer had a role to play. Our destination from here on is no longer something you can perceive from one set point of view.

Naturally, if the world were only full of selfish people like me we'd be in a bit of trouble. But to return to the earlier example I gave, we need to be able to skillfully use both the small and the large kettles in the kitchen. Human intelligence, or perhaps common sense, necessitates different approaches for different purposes. Society runs smoothly and, in a good sense, efficiently only when diverse systems of thought and world views unite. In a word, the system becomes more refined and sophisticated.

Of course in every society you need consensus. Without that a society can't exist. At the same time, though, we need to value the relatively small number of *exceptions* that lie outside the general consensus, and make sure we take those into consideration. In a mature society that kind of balance is an essential element. And within that balance, society will give birth to a new kind of depth and self-reflection. But looking at present-day Japan, it doesn't appear that we've turned the rudder much in that direction.

TAKE, FOR INSTANCE, the Fukushima nuclear-power-plant accident of March 2011. As I followed the reports about it, I was led to the depressing conclusion that this was, fundamentally, an inevitable manmade disaster caused by the Japanese social system. And I imagine many of you, too, came to the same conclusion.

The nuclear-power-plant accident drove tens of thousands of people out of their hometowns, with no hope in sight of ever returning. It's such a sad situation. The direct cause of this was a natural catastrophe that exceeded anything people could imagine, and a series of unfortunate coincidences. But what really pushed this to the level of a fatal tragedy was, in my view, structural flaws inherent in the existing system, and the distortions these created. The lack of responsibility within the larger system, and the failure of the ability to make decisions. An evil efficiency that had lost any sense of vision and that could not *imagine* other people's pain.

Based almost entirely on the argument that nuclear power is economical, the nation pushed through a policy of reliance on nuclear energy—but the potential risk (and the actual risks that did surface off and on) were intentionally concealed. And now we're the ones who have to pay the price. If we don't shine a light on this full-steam-ahead attitude that permeates our social system, and reveal all the problems and make some fundamental corrections, I'm afraid that the same kind of tragedy will occur all over again somewhere.

There is a point, perhaps, to the argument that for Japan, a country with limited resources, nuclear power is necessary. I am, in principle, opposed to nuclear power, but if it could be scrupulously managed by trustworthy supervisors, and the operation could be strictly overseen by a competent third-party organization, and all information accurately disseminated to the public, then *perhaps* there would be room for discussion. But when nuclear-power facilities that have the capacity to produce lethal damage, when a dangerous system that could destroy a country (and it's true that the Chernobyl accident was one factor in the fall of the Soviet Union) is managed by commercial corporations that prioritize numbers and efficiency over everything else, and when this is all *led* and *supervised* by a bureaucracy built on rote memorization and top-down decision making, one that lacks any sympathy toward humanity, then you can be sure that very serious risks will arise. And the consequences may pollute the land, destroy nature, damage people's health, forfeit the nation's trust, and destroy the environment people live in. And it's not just "may," since these very things have all *actually happened* in Fukushima.

I'VE GONE ON a bit of a tangent here, but the point is that the contradictions inherent in the Japanese education system are directly linked to the contradictions in Japanese society. Or perhaps it's the opposite. At any rate, we've gotten to the point where we no longer have the luxury to simply turn a blind eye to these contradictions.

Let me return to the topic of schools.

When I was going to school, from the late 1950s through the 1960s, school bullying and children refusing to attend school were not such major problems. This isn't to say that there weren't any problems in schools then or in the education system (I think there were lots of problems), but at least I myself hardly saw any cases around me of bullying or school truancy. Not that there weren't any, but it wasn't that huge a problem then.

I think this was because in this period not long after the war, the country was relatively poor, and people had clear-cut goals to work for—namely, *recovery* and *development*. Even if there were contradictions in the system, the overall mood was upbeat. That sort of trend had an unseen effect on the children. On an everyday level, negative psychological moments didn't have such a huge influence on children's lives. There was a kind of basically optimistic feeling that as long as we stuck with it, any problems and contradictions would gradually disappear. So for me, too, even though I didn't like school so much, I took going to school for granted, and did my best to attend every day without really questioning it.

Nowadays, though, bullying and truancy have become major social issues, and rarely a day goes by without a report on them in the media. And quite a few children who are bullied end up taking their own lives. It's nothing less than tragic. Lots of people give lots of opinions about these problems, and there have been all sorts of policies developed to deal with them, but it doesn't look like this trend is going to improve anytime soon.

And it's not just bullying among students. There are some major issues with teachers as well. This happened quite a while ago, but there was an incident at a school in Kobe where a teacher shut the heavy front gate to the school right when the bell rang for classes to start, and a female student got caught in the gate and died. "Tardiness has become rampant these days at our school, so we were compelled to do this," the teacher explained in his defense. Nobody applauds tardiness, of course, but clearly there is a major difference between being on time to school and a person's life.

In this teacher's mind, the narrow sense of purpose he took from *zero tolerance for lateness* became an obsession to the point where he lost a balanced view of the world. And a sense of balance is an important quality for educators. In newspapers there were comments from parents to the effect that "he was a good teacher, very devoted to education." There has to be something wrong with anyone uttering—or even being able to utter—a statement like that. What about the pain of the person who was crushed to death?

I can imagine schools metaphorically crushing down students, but schools physically crushing students to death boggles my mind.

Needless to say, this pathological situation (I think it's okay to call it that) at schools is nothing less than a projection of the pathology of the social system. If society as a whole has a natural vitality, with clear-cut goals, then even if there are some problems in the educational system, they can somehow be overcome by the power inherent there. However, if society loses its energy, and there's a widespread sense of hopelessness, this will show up most prominently, and have the greatest effect, in the educational arena. In schools, in classrooms. Like canaries in coal mines, children are the ones who are most sensitive to, and first to detect, the corrupt air.

As I mentioned earlier, when I was a child, society itself had room for growth, so that there was room for conflicts between the individual and the system, and as a result they did not turn into major social problems. Because of this societal flexibility, there was a space for all kinds of contradictions and frustrations. Or to put it another way, there was room to retreat when you were troubled. But now, after the period of rapid growth and the bubble economy is over, it's difficult to find a place of refuge like that. Thinking that everything will work out if you just go with the flow no longer exists as a solution.

A society in which there is not enough room to escape produces deep problems in the educational arena, and necessitates new solutions. First of all we have to create a place where these solutions might be found.

What kind of place would that be?

It would be a place where the individual and the larger system can each move freely, and gently interact and negotiate with one another. In other words, a place where each person can freely stretch out their arms and legs and take a good, long breath. A place apart from hierarchy, efficiency, and bullying. Simply put, a warm, temporary shelter. One that anyone can enter and is free to leave. A serene middle ground between individual and community. Whatever position one takes up in it is left up to the person's discretion. I'd like to call it a *space of individual recovery*.

It can be a small space at first. It doesn't have to be anything big. A compact, handmade sort of place where all kinds of possibilities can actually be tried out, and if something works, it can become a model or springboard and then develop further. That space can gradually be extended even more. That's the way I see it. It might take time, but I think that's the most correct and rational way to go. It would be great if these spaces could spring up spontaneously everywhere.

But these spaces need to form organically. The worst-case scenario would be if an entity like the Ministry of Education tried to force it. Since what we're advocating is a *space of individual recovery*, having the country institutionally try to solve the issue would be getting the priorities wrong, and it would end up a total farce.

IN MY OWN CASE, when I look back to when I was in school, the biggest saving grace for me was having some close friends, and reading tons of books.

When it came to books, I greedily devoured a wide range, like I was busily shoveling coal into a blazing furnace. I was so busy every day enjoying one book after another, digesting them (in many cases *not* properly digesting them), that I didn't have any time left to think about anything else. Sometimes I think that might actually have been a good thing for me. If I had looked at the situation around me more, thought deeply about the unnatural, contradictory, and deceitful things there and plunged right into pursuing things I couldn't accept, I might have been driven into a dead end and suffered because of it.

Also, reading so widely helped to *relativize* my point of view, and I think that was very significant for me back when I was a teenager. I experienced all the emotions depicted in books almost as if they were my own; in my imagination I traveled freely through time and space, saw all kinds of amazing sights, and let all kinds of words pass right through my very body. Through all this, my perspective on life became a more composite view. In other words, I wasn't gazing at the world just from the spot where I was standing, but was able to take a step back and take a more panoramic view.

If you always see things from your own standpoint, the world shrinks. Your body gets stiff, your footwork grows heavy, and you can no longer move. But if you're able to view where you're standing from other perspectives—to put it another way, if you can entrust your existence to some other system—the world will grow more three-dimensional, more supple. And I believe that as long as we live in this world, that kind of agile stance is extremely important. In my life this has been one of the biggest rewards of reading.

If there hadn't been any books, or if I hadn't read so many, I think my life would have been far drearier. For me, then, the act of reading was its own kind of essential school. A customized school built and run just for me, one in which I learned so many important lessons. A place where there were no tiresome rules or regulations, no numerical evaluations, no angling for the top spot. And, of course, no bullying. While I was part of a larger system, I was able to secure another, more personal system of my own.

The mental image I have of a *space of individual recovery* is exactly like that. It's not limited just to reading. Even for kids who

can't adjust to the actual school system, the ones who aren't especially interested in studying, if they are able to find their own customized *space of individual recovery*, and can discover something
there that fits them in order to develop possibilities at their own
pace, they'll be able to naturally overcome the *wall of the system*. In
order for this to happen, though, there has to be support from the
community and family, and an understanding and appreciation of
this way of thinking

Both my parents taught Japanese (my mother quit teaching
after she got married), and they never complained about me reading books. They were a little displeased with my academic record,
but never told me to stop reading all the time and study for exams.
Or maybe they did sometimes, but I have no memory of it. That's
about the extent of what they would have said. I'm grateful to them
for that.

I'LL SAY IT AGAIN, but I never had much affection
for the "system" called school. I did have a few great teachers, and
I did learn some important things, but this was nearly all canceled
out by the fact that almost all the classes and lectures were boring.
So mind-numbingly boring that when I finished school I thought
I'd had a lifetime's worth of boredom. But no matter how much I
might think this, in our lives one boring thing after another flutters
down at us from the sky, and wells up from the ground.

People who absolutely love school, and feel sad when they can't
go, probably won't become novelists. I say this because a novelist is
a person who steadily fills his head with a world of his own. When
I was in class, I didn't pay much attention to the lesson, and instead
was lost in all sorts of daydreams. If I were a child today, I might

have trouble fitting in and might end up one of the many kids who refuse to attend. But as I said, when I was young, truancy was not a trend yet, and I don't think we even had the idea that not attending school was a choice.

In every age, in every society, imagination plays a crucial role.

One opposite of imagination is "efficiency." And one of the factors that drove tens of thousands of people from their homes in Fukushima was this very "efficiency." The notion that nuclear-power generation is efficient energy and is good for the community, and the lie cooked up out of the notion—namely, the so-called safety myth—brought this tragic situation, this unrecoverable disaster, upon our nation. It's fair to say that this was a defeat for our imagination. But even now it's not too late. We have to establish an axis of free thought and individual ideas that can counter this short-circuited, dangerous set of values. And then extend this ideological axis to the broader community.

This isn't to say that I hope school education simply "enriches children's imagination." I'm not hoping for that much. When all is said and done, the ones who will enrich children's imaginations are children themselves. Not teachers, not educational facilities. And certainly not educational policies of the country or local government. Not all children have a rich imagination. Just like some children are fast runners and others are not. Some children have a rich imagination, and others—though no doubt they display amazing talents in other areas—aren't what you'd called very imaginative. It's only to be expected. That's society. If "Let's enrich children's imagination" becomes a set goal, though, then things will go bad all over again.

What I hope for from schools is simply that they do not suppress the imagination of children who are naturally imaginative. That's enough. I want them to provide an environment in which each person's individuality can thrive. Do that, and schools will become fuller, freer places. Simultaneously, society itself will also become a fuller, freer place.

As one novelist, those are my thoughts. Not that my thinking about this will change anything.

What Kind of Characters
Should I Include?

↳

'M OFTEN ASKED if any characters in my novels are based on real people. On the whole, the answer is *no*, though sometimes it's *yes*. I've written a lot of novels, but only two or three times have I intentionally, from the start, had a real person in mind when I created a character. When I did, I was a bit nervous that somebody might detect that the character was modeled on somebody—especially if the person who did was the one the character was based on (in all cases they were secondary characters in the novels)—but fortunately no one's ever pointed that out, not even once. I might model the character after a real person, but

I always carefully and diligently rework the character so people won't recognize him. Probably the person himself doesn't, either.

What happens more often is that people claim that the characters I haven't based on anyone, the imaginary ones I totally made up, are modeled after real people. In some cases there are even people who swear that a certain character is based on them. Somerset Maugham was actually sued by a person he'd never met and never even heard of, who claimed that one of Maugham's novels was based on him. In the novel Maugham depicted each of the characters in a very vivid, real way, in some cases quite nastily (or, to put a better spin on it, satirically), which made the person's reaction even more intense. When he read Maugham's skillful depictions of the characters, this person must have felt he was being personally criticized and belittled.

In most cases, the characters who appear in my novels naturally emerge from the flow of the story. Except for a few rare cases, I never decide ahead of time that I'll present a certain type of character. As I write, a kind of axis emerges that makes it possible for the appearance of certain characters, and I go ahead and add one detail after another as I see fit, like iron scraps attach to a magnet. And in this way an overall picture of a person emerges. Afterwards I often think that certain details bear a resemblance of sorts to a real person, but I never start out thinking I'll use an aspect of a real person to create a character. Most of the process happens automatically. In other words, as I create the character, I think it's more that I almost unconsciously pull out information and various fragments from the cabinets in my brain and then weave them together.

I have my own name for this automatic process: the Automatic Dwarves. I've almost always driven stick-shift cars, and the first time I drove an automatic, I had a feeling like *there must be dwarves living inside the gear box, each in charge of operating a separate gear.* And I also had a faint anxiety that someday those dwarves would decide they'd had enough of slaving away for someone else, stop work, and go on strike, and my car would suddenly stop working right in the middle of the highway.

I know you'll laugh to hear me say this, but when it comes to the process of creating characters it's like those Automatic Dwarves living in my unconscious are, despite a bit of grumbling, somehow managing to work hard. And all I do is diligently copy it all down. Naturally what I write isn't neatly organized as a ready-to-go novel, so later I rework it a number of times, changing its form. That rewriting process is more conscious and logical. But the creation of the prototype is an unconscious and intuitive process. There's no choice, really. I have to do it this way or my characters will turn out unnatural and dead. That's why, in the beginning stage of the process, I leave everything up to these Automatic Dwarves.

IN ANY CASE, in the same way that you have to read a lot of books in order to write novels, to write about people you need to know a lot of them.

By "know" I don't mean you have to comprehend them, or go so far as to *really understand* them deep down. All you need to do is glance at the person's appearance, how they talk and act, their special characteristics. Those people you like, ones you're not so fond of, ones that, frankly, you dislike—it's important to observe people without, as much as possible, choosing which ones you observe. What I mean is, if the only people you put in your novels are the kind you like, ones you're interested in or can easily understand, then your novels, ultimately, will lack a certain expansiveness.

There are all sorts of different people, doing all sorts of different actions, and it's through that clash of difference that things get moving and the story is propelled forward. So you shouldn't just avert your eyes when you decide you can't stomach somebody, but instead ask yourself "What is it I don't like about them?" and "Why don't I like that?" Those are the main points to keep in mind.

A long time ago—I think I was in my mid-thirties—someone told me, "There are never any bad people in your novels." (Later on I learned that Kurt Vonnegut was told the same thing by his father just before his father passed away.) I could see the point. Ever since then, I've consciously tried to include more negative characters in my novels. But things didn't work out as I'd hoped. Back then, I was more inclined toward the creation of a private world—one that was, if anything, harmonious—than creating large-scale narrative-driven books. I had to build my own neat little world as a shelter from the harsh realities of the larger world around me.

But as time has passed and I've matured, you might say (as a person and as a writer), I've ever so gradually been able to include more negative characters in the stories I write, characters that introduce an element of discord. I've been able to do this first of all because the novelistic world I've created has taken shape more and functions fairly well, so as a next step my project was to make this world broader and deeper, and more dynamic than before. Doing that meant adding more variety to my characters and expanding the scope of their actions. I keenly felt the need to do this.

Additionally, I'd experienced many things in my life. At age thirty I became a professional writer, with a public presence, and like it or not had to face a lot of pressure. I don't naturally gravitate to the spotlight, but there were times when, reluctantly, I was forced to put myself there. Sometimes I had to do things that I didn't want to do, or was very disappointed when a person I was close to spoke out against me. Some people would praise me with words they didn't really feel, while others—pointlessly, as far as I can see it—heaped ridicule on me. And others spoke half-truths about me. Additionally, I went through other experiences I can only characterize as strange and out of the ordinary.

Every time I went through these negative experiences, I tried to observe in detail the way the people involved looked and how they spoke and acted. If I'm going to have to go through all this, I figured, I should at least get something useful out of it (to get back what I put into it, you could say). Naturally these experiences hurt me, even made me depressed sometimes, but now I feel they provided a lot of nourishment for me as a novelist. Of course, I had plenty of wonderful, enjoyable experiences as well, but for whatever reason the ones I recall now are the negative ones. It's the unpleasant memories that remain, the ones I don't want to remember. Perhaps there's more to learn from them.

When I think about it, I realize that the novels I enjoy most are the ones with lots of fascinating supporting characters. The one that leaps to mind is Dostoevsky's *Demons*. If you've read it, you know what I mean; there are plenty of oddball minor characters throughout the novel. It's a long novel but holds my interest to the end. One colorful, weird character after another appears, the kind that makes you wonder, "Why *this* kind of person?" Dostoevsky must have been someone with a huge mental cabinet to work with.

In Japanese literature the novels of Natsume Sōseki contain all kinds of appealing, colorful characters. Even the ones who only appear briefly are vividly portrayed and unique. A line they might utter, or an expression or action of theirs, will strangely linger in the mind. What impresses me about Sōseki's novels is that there's hardly ever any makeshift character, one that is there because the author decided he needed that sort of person to appear at that point. These are novels not created by the mind but rather through sensations and experience. Sōseki paid his dues in each and every line, and you feel a sort of peace of mind as you read them.

One of the things I most enjoy about writing novels is the sense that *I can become anybody I want to be.*

I started off by writing novels in the first person, using the first-person male pronoun *boku*, and continued in the same vein for some twenty years. Occasionally I'd write short stories in third person, but my novels were consistently in first person. Naturally this "I" didn't equal me, Haruki Murakami (just like Philip Marlowe isn't Raymond Chandler), and in each novel the image of the first-person male protagonist changes, but as I continued writing in first person, the line between the real-life me and the protagonist of the novels to a certain extent inevitably blurred, both for the writer and for the reader.

This wasn't a problem at first, since creating and expanding a novelistic world by using a fictionalized version of "I" was my original aim, but over time I gradually got the sense that I needed more. Especially as my novels got longer, using only the first-person narrative felt confining and stifling. In *Hard-Boiled Wonderland and the End of the World* I used two versions of "I" (using the pronouns *boku* and *watakushi* in alternating chapters), which I think was an attempt to break through the functional limits of a first-person narrative.

The Wind-Up Bird Chronicle (1994–95) was the last novel I

wrote solely in first person.* But when a novel is as long as that book, you can't make do just with the viewpoint of one first-person "I"; so throughout the novel I incorporated a number of other novelistic devices, such as other people's stories, long letters, etc. I introduced all kinds of narrative techniques in order to break through the structural limitations of first-person narration. Even with all that, though, I felt I couldn't take it any further—so with my next novel, *Kafka on the Shore* (2002), I changed to writing half of it in third person. The chapters about the boy Kafka were written in the usual first-person "I" narrative, but the remaining chapters were in third person. Sort of a compromise, you might say, but even just introducing the third-person voice in half the novel opened up my novelistic world considerably. At least as I wrote this novel I felt, on a technical level, much freer than when I wrote *The Wind-Up Bird Chronicle*.

The short-story collection *Tokyo Kitanshu* and the medium-length novel *After Dark,* which I wrote after this, were from start to finish in purely third person. It was like I was making sure that in these formats—short stories and a medium-length novel—I could do a solid job of employing third-person narrative. Like taking a new sports car you just bought out for a spin on a mountain road to see what it can do. By following these steps in the process, it took some twenty years since I first debuted to say farewell to the first person and begin to write solely in third person. Quite a long stretch of time.

* Editor's Note: Haruki Murakami subsequently published *Killing Commendatore* in 2017 (with an English-language translation in 2018), another novel written in the first person.

Why did it take so long to change the voice I wrote in? Even I don't know the exact reason. I can say that my body and psyche had grown completely used to the process of writing novels with an "I" first person, so it took some time to make the switch. For me it was not simply a change from first-person narrative but close to a fundamental transformation in my standpoint as a writer.

I'M THE TYPE OF PERSON who needs time to change the way I do things. For instance, for a long time I couldn't give names to my characters. Nicknames like "Rat" or "J" were fine, because I just couldn't give them actual names. Why not? I don't know the answer. All I can say is that I felt embarrassed about assigning people names. I felt that somebody like me endowing others (even if they're fictional characters I made up) with names seemed kind of phony. Maybe in the beginning I felt embarrassed, too, about the whole act itself of writing novels. It was like laying my naked heart out for everyone to see.

I was finally able to give the main characters names starting with the novel *Norwegian Wood* (1987). Until then, for the eight years prior, I basically used characters without names, and wrote in first person. If you think about it, I imposed a pretty restricted, round-about system on myself, but at the time it didn't bother me much. I just thought, "That's how it is."

But as my novels became longer and more complex, I started to feel it was inconvenient not to have names for the characters. If you have a lot of characters and they don't have names, it can cause all kinds of real confusion. So I resigned myself to it and made the decision, as I was writing *Norwegian Wood,* that I would *name* the characters. It wasn't easy, but I closed my eyes, steeled myself, and after that it wasn't all that hard to give my characters names. Nowadays I'm able to easily come up with names. With *Colorless Tsukuru Tazaki and His Years of Pilgrimage* there's even a character's name in the title. With *1Q84* it was at the point that I came up with the name "Aomame" for the female protagonist that the story really started to take off. In that sense names have become an important element in my novels.

In this way, every time I write a new novel I tell myself, "Okay, this time, here is what I'm going to try to accomplish," one by one setting up concrete goals for myself—for the most part visible, technical types of goals. I enjoy writing like that. As I clear a new hurdle and accomplish something new or different, I get a real sense that I've grown, even if it's a little, as a writer. It's like climbing, step by step, up a ladder. The wonderful thing about being a novelist is that even in your fifties and sixties, that kind of growth and innovation is possible. There's no age limit. The same wouldn't hold true for an athlete.

By using third person, increasing the number of characters, and giving them names, the possibilities for my novels expanded. In other words, I could include all types and shades of people with all sorts of opinions and worldviews, and depict the diverse intertwining among them. And what's most wonderful of all is that I can *become almost anyone I want*. Even when I was writing in first person, I had that feeling, but with third person the choices are far greater.

When I write in first person, in most cases I roughly take the protagonist (or narrator) as myself in a broad sense. This isn't the *real me*, as I've said, but change the situation and circumstances and it might be. By branching out, I am able to divide myself. And by dividing myself like that and throwing myself into the narrative, I am able to verify who I am, and pinpoint the point of contact between myself and others, or between myself and the world. In the beginning that way of writing really suited me. And most of the novels I loved were also written in first person.

For instance, *The Great Gatsby* is in first person. The hero of the novel is Jay Gatsby, but the narrator is always the young man Nick Carraway. Through the subtle interplay between the first-person narrator (Nick) and Gatsby, and through dramatic developments in the story, Fitzgerald is actually narrating the truth about himself. That viewpoint lends depth to the story.

However, the fact that the story is narrated from Nick's viewpoint means the novel takes on certain realistic limits. It's difficult for the story to reflect things that happen outside of where Nick can perceive them. Fitzgerald employed all sorts of methods, mobilizing every novelistic technique there is to skillfully overcome those limitations. Those are fascinating in and of themselves, but even those technical devices have their own limitations. And in fact, Fitzgerald never again wrote a novel structured like *The Great Gatsby*.

J. D. Salinger's *The Catcher in the Rye*, too, is very artfully written, an outstanding first-person novel, but he likewise never wrote a novel in this style again. My guess is that both authors were afraid that the constraints of that structure might make them wind up writing essentially the same novel all over again. And I think that decision of theirs was probably the correct one.

With series novels, like Raymond Chandler's Marlowe novels, the "narrowness" of these limitations can be employed to—

conversely—effectively lend a kind of intimate predictability (my early "Rat" stories perhaps had a touch of this). But with stand-alone novels, in many cases the restrictive wall that the first-person narration constructs makes it increasingly stifling for the writer. Which is exactly why I tried, from many angles, to shake up the first-person narrative in order to carve out new territory, but with *The Wind-Up Bird Chronicle* I realized I'd reached the limits of what I could do with it.

In *Kafka on the Shore* I introduced third-person narrative in half of the story, and I found a real relief in writing the story that paralleled Kafka's, the story of the odd old man Nakata and Hoshino, the somewhat uncouth young truck driver. In writing this section, at the same time I was dividing myself so that I could project myself onto others. More precisely, I could *entrust others with my divided self.* And as a result, the various possible combinations increased substantially. And the narrative could intricately divide and expand in all sorts of directions.

I can hear people saying, "If that's the case, then you should have switched to third person long ago—then you would have improved much faster," but actually I couldn't work things out that simply. The thing is, personality-wise I'm not that adaptable, and changing my novelistic standpoint involves making a major structural change to my novels. In order to support this transformation, I needed to acquire some solid novelistic techniques and fundamental physical stamina. Which is why I did it gradually, seeing how it went, making this change only in stages. When it comes to the body, I had to slowly alter my frame and muscles to fit my workout goals. And it takes time and effort to reshape your body.

AT ANY RATE, by the early 2000s, I'd mastered a new vehicle, third-person narrative, and could step into uncharted territory in my novels. I felt liberated, as if a wall that had been there had suddenly disappeared.

It goes without saying that characters are a critical element in novels. The novelist has to put characters in his novel that have a sense of reality, yet are interesting and speak and act in ways that are a bit unpredictable, and make them a central, or close to central, part of it. A novel with predictable characters who only say and do predictable things isn't going to attract many readers. Naturally there will be people who say that novels in which ordinary characters do ordinary things are the really outstanding ones, but for me (and this is, after all, just my personal preference), I can't get interested in those kinds of books.

But beyond being real, interesting, and somewhat unpredictable, I think what's more important is the question of how far the novel's characters advance the story. Of course it's the writer who creates the characters; but characters who are—in a real sense—alive will eventually break free of the writer's control and begin to act independently. I'm not the only one who feels this—many fiction writers acknowledge it. In fact, unless that phenomenon occurs, writing the novel becomes a strained, painful, and trying process. When a novel is on the right track, characters take on a life of their own, the story moves forward by itself, and a very happy situation evolves whereby the novelist just ends up writing down what he sees happening in front of him. And in some cases the character takes the novelist by the hand and leads him or her to an unexpected destination.

To give an example, I'll cite one from a recent novel, *Colorless Tsukuru Tazaki and His Years of Pilgrimage*, in which there's a very attractive woman character, Sara Kimoto. Truthfully, I started writing this novel intending it to be a short story. I expected it to be only about sixty pages in length in Japanese manuscript pages.

To sum up the storyline, Tsukuru Tazaki, the main character, had four really good friends from high school in Nagoya who suddenly told him they didn't want to see him or hear from him ever again. They don't give a reason, and he doesn't venture to ask for one. He goes off to college in Tokyo, gets a job at a railway company, and is thirty-six in the present time of the story. Having his best friends from high school cut him off like that without ever giving a reason has left him deeply wounded. But he hides this pain and lives a peaceful everyday life. His work goes well, he gets along with the people around him, and he's had several girlfriends along the way. Still, he hasn't had any deep emotional attachment to anyone. At this point he meets Sara, who is two years older than he is, and they start seeing each other.

On a whim he tells Sara about being cut off by his four close friends from high school. Sara ponders this, then tells him he has to go back to Nagoya and find out what happened eighteen years before to cause this rift. "Not to see what you want to see, but what you *must* see," she tells him.

To tell the truth, until she said that, the idea that Tsukuru needed to go back to see his four friends was the farthest thought from my mind. I'd been planning to write a fairly short story in which Tsukuru lives a quiet, mysterious life, never knowing why he'd been rejected like that. But once she said that (and I merely wrote down what she said to him), I had to make Tsukuru go to Nagoya and, in the end, send him all the way to Finland. And I needed to then explore those four characters, Tsukuru's former friends, all over again to show what sort of people they were. And give details of the lives they'd led up to this point. As a result, what started as a short story quite naturally turned into a novel.

In other words, in almost an instant, the words that Sara spoke completely changed the story's direction, character, scope, and structure. This was a complete surprise to me. If you think about it, she wasn't saying that to the protagonist, Tsukuru Tazaki, so much as to me, the author. "You have to write more about this," she was saying to me. "You've stepped into that realm and you've acquired enough strength to do that." So Sara was, again, perhaps a reflection of my alter ego, one aspect of my consciousness telling me not to stop at the place where I'd intended. "You have to delve deeper into this, write more about it," she was saying. In that sense *Colorless Tsukuru Tazaki and His Years of Pilgrimage* is a work that holds no small significance for me. On a formal level it's a *realistic novel*, yet I find that there are all sorts of intricate, metaphorical things going on below the surface.

The characters in my novels urge me—the writer—to go on, and they encourage me to forge ahead. I felt this keenly when I was writing *1Q84* in the words and actions of Aomame. It was as if she were forcibly expanding something inside of me. Looking back on it, it seems that most of the time it's female characters, not male characters, who lead me and spur me on. Why that is, I have no idea.

What I want to say is that in a certain sense, while the novelist is creating a novel, he is simultaneously being created by the novel as well.

I'm sometimes asked, "Why don't you write novels with characters the same age as yourself?" I'm in my mid-sixties now, in 2015, so the question is, why don't you write stories with characters that age? Why don't you write about the lives of those kinds of people? Isn't that a natural job of a writer?

But there's one thing I don't understand, which is, why is it *necessary* that a writer write about people the same age as him? Why is that a "natural job"? As I said before, one of the things I enjoy the most about writing novels is being able to become anyone I want. So why should I, on my own, give up such a wonderful right?

When I wrote *Kafka on the Shore* I was a little past fifty years old, yet I made the main character a fifteen-year-old boy. And all the time I was writing I felt like I was a fifteen-year-old. Of course these weren't the "feelings" a present-day fifteen-year-old boy would be feeling. Instead I transferred the feelings I had back when *I was fifteen* onto a fictional "present." Still, as I wrote the novel, I was able to vividly relive inside me, almost as they were, the air I actually breathed at age fifteen, the light I actually saw. Through the power of writing I could draw out sensations and feelings that had long lain hidden deep inside. It was a truly wonderful experience. Perhaps the sort of sensation only a novelist can taste.

But just me enjoying this by myself will not create a literary work. It has to be relativized. In other words, put into a form so readers can share that pleasure. Which is why I included the character Nakata, an "old man" in his sixties. Nakata was also, in a sense, my alter ego, a projection of me. And by having Kafka and Nakata act in parallel and in response to each other, the novel acquired a healthy balance. At least I felt that way as the author—and I feel that way even now.

Maybe someday I will write a novel with a protagonist my own age, but at this point I don't feel it's *absolutely necessary*. What pops up first for me is the idea for a novel. Then the story naturally, spontaneously reaches out from the idea. As I said in the beginning, it's the story itself that decides what sort of characters will appear. It's not something I think about and decide on ahead of time. As the writer, I merely follow directions as a faithful scribe.

I might, at one time, become a twenty-year-old lesbian. Another time I'll be a thirty-year-old unemployed househusband. I put my feet into the shoes I'm given then, make my foot size fit those shoes, and then start to act. That's all it is. I don't make the shoes fit my foot size but, rather, make my feet fit the shoes. It's not something you can do in reality, but if you toil for years as a novelist, you find you're able to accomplish it. The reason being that it's all imaginary. And being imaginary, it's like things that take place in dreams. In dreams—whether ones you have while asleep or dreams you have while awake—you have hardly any choice about it. Basically I just go with the flow. And as long as I'm following that flow I can freely do all sorts of things that are *hardly possible*. This is indeed one of the main joys of writing novels.

Every time I'm asked "Why don't you write novels with characters the same age as yourself?" that's how I want to reply, but it's too long an explanation, and I doubt people would easily get it, so I always give some suitably vague reply. I smile and say something like "Good question. Maybe someday I'll do just that."

But aside from this—aside from whether or not I'll put them in a novel—in the ordinary sense it's an extremely difficult task to observe *yourself as you are now*, objectively and accurately. To grasp yourself in the present progressive form is not easy. Maybe that's precisely why I wear all kinds of shoes *that aren't mine.* Through that I'm able to discover myself in a more comprehensive way, much like triangulating a location.

At any rate, there still seems so much I need to learn about the characters in my novels. And at the same time there seems to be so much I need to learn *from* the characters in my novels. In the future, I want my novels to bring to life all kinds of weird, eccentric, and colorful characters. Whenever I begin writing a new novel, I get excited, wondering what kind of people I'm going to meet next.

Who Do I Write For?

NTERVIEWERS SOMETIMES ASK ME, "What sort of readers do you have in mind when you write your novels?" And I'm always sort of stuck for an answer. The reason being that I've never had the sense that I'm writing *for someone else*. And I don't particularly have that feeling even now.

It's true in a sense to say that I write for myself. Particularly with my first novel, *Hear the Wind Sing*, one that I wrote late at night at my kitchen table, I had no thought at all that ordinary readers would ever see it, and (truly) all I thought about as I wrote it was that writing made me *feel good*. Taking some images I had inside me, choosing words that satisfied me, putting those words together into sentences—that's all I had in my mind at the time. But what sort of people might someday read this novel, whether they would feel drawn to it, what sort of literary message might be contained within it—I didn't have the time to consider any of that, and there was no need to. It was a simple thing, really, very pristine.

When I was writing this first book there was also a sense of it being therapeutic. All creative activity is, to some extent, done partly with the intention to rectify or fix yourself. In other words, by relativizing yourself, by adapting your soul to a form that's different from what it is now, you can resolve—or sublimate—the contradictions, rifts, and distortions that inevitably crop up in the process of being alive. And if things go well, this effect can be shared with readers. Though I wasn't specifically conscious of it at the time, I think I was instinctively seeking that kind of self-cleansing action. Which is why, in a very unselfconscious way, I started wanting to write novels in the first place.

But after that first novel won a newcomers award sponsored by a literary magazine, was published as a book, sold a bit, and was reviewed fairly well, and I was given the label "novelist," I was, whether I wanted to be or not, compelled to start thinking about *readers*. My book was now lined up on shelves in bookstores, my name boldly printed on the cover, with the general public now reading it, so a certain tension inevitably began to color my writing. Which doesn't mean that my basic stance of writing to enjoy myself had changed very much. I figured that as long as I enjoyed what I wrote, there had to be readers somewhere who also enjoyed reading it. Maybe not all that many, but that was fine with me. If I could communicate meaningfully with them, then that was all I needed.

My next novel, *Pinball, 1973,* and then my short-story collections *A Slow Boat to China* and *A Perfect Day for Kangaroos* were all written with that sort of optimistic, easygoing attitude. At the time I had a full-time day job and was able to get by okay on that income. Novels were, so to speak, more a hobby I wrote in my spare time.

One well-known literary critic (who is no longer alive) gave a scathing review of my first novel, *Hear the Wind Sing,* saying, "You're in big trouble if you think this kind of thing passes for literature." When I read this, I simply thought, "Okay, I guess some people feel that way." It didn't make me upset or want to lash back. That critic and I had a very different way of viewing *literature.* What kind of ideological content my works had, what social role they played, whether they were avant-garde or reactionary, artistic fiction or not—I'd never given any of this a single thought. I'd started out with the stance that if I enjoy writing it, that's sufficient; so from the start our ideas didn't mesh. In *Hear the Wind Sing* I introduced a fictional writer named Derek Hartfield, one of whose novels is entitled *What's Wrong About Feeling Good?* And that was exactly the way I felt about it at the time. What's wrong about feeling good?

Looking back at it now, it seems a simplistic, slapdash way of thinking, but I was very young then (in my early thirties), the upheaval of the student movement was still fresh in my mind, and I had maintained a pretty disobedient attitude—an antithetical, defiant, resistant stance toward authority and the establishment. (Perhaps a bit impertinent and childish, granted, though things worked out okay.)

That attitude gradually began to transform around the time I started writing *A Wild Sheep Chase* (1982). I was growing aware that if I just kept up this "What's wrong about feeling good?" attitude, as a professional writer I'd probably write myself into a corner. Even my readers who enjoyed my writing style, and found it "innovative," would, though, soon tire of reading the same sort of thing. "What? This again?" they'd think. And of course as the one who writes the books, I'd get fed up with it, too.

And it wasn't like I was dying to write that style of novel. It's just that I didn't have the technical writing skills yet to directly come to grips with a lengthy novel, and could only, at this point, write in that sort of style that stepped lightly. And that airy way of writing just happened to strike some people as fresh and new. For me, though, since I'd made the leap to being a novelist, I wanted to write a novel that was a little deeper, more expansive in scope. But "deep" and "expansive" didn't mean I wanted to write in a formally literary, or mainstream-fiction, kind of way. I wanted to write a novel that made me feel good writing it, a novel that had the power to break down the front door. I wanted to do more than just take images inside me and express them in words in a fragmentary, instinctive way; I wanted to come to grips with the ideas and awareness inside me and in a more comprehensive, three-dimensional way set them down in writing.

The year before I made this decision, I read Ryū Murakami's novel *Coin Locker Babies* and was really blown away. But this was something only Ryū Murakami could write. I also read some of Kenji Nakagami's novels and was really impressed, but again only Nakagami could have written them. They were both different from what I wanted to write. I had to carve out my own path, and with the example of these powerful works in mind, I knew I had to write the kind of novel that only I could write.

And so I proceeded to start writing *A Wild Sheep Chase* as a kind of answer to these propositions. I wanted to make the novel itself as deep and profound as I could without making my style any heavier, or harming the *good feelings* (or, to put it another way, without incorporating it into the system of pure literature). That was my basic idea. And to do that I had to proactively introduce the framework of narrative into the novel. This was very clear to me. Making narrative central would make it, inevitably, a work that took longer to complete. Unlike my previous works, it wasn't something I could complete in the snatches of free time between my day job. So before I began writing *A Wild Sheep Chase* I sold the jazz club I'd been running, and became a so-called full-time writer. At the time my income from the jazz club exceeded my income writing, but I took the plunge anyway and gave up the business. I wanted my life to focus on writing novels, and devote all the time I had to writing. A bit of an exaggeration, perhaps, but it was step from which there was no turning back, a sort of burning of bridges.

Almost everyone I knew was against this decision, claiming I shouldn't rush into things. My café was doing good business at the time, with a steady income, and they felt it was a waste to give that up. "Can't you let someone else run the shop while you write novels?" they asked. Most of them probably didn't expect I'd be able to earn a living just writing novels. But I had no doubts. I've always been the type who, when he does something, plunges in headfirst. My personality just wouldn't allow me to *let someone else run the shop*. This was a crucial moment in my life. I needed to make a firm decision and stick by it. Even if it was just one time, I wanted to use everything I had to focus on writing a novel. If it didn't work out, then so be it. I could start all over again. Those were my thoughts then. I sold the café and gave up my apartment in Tokyo in order to concentrate on writing. I left the city, started going to bed early and getting up early, and began running every day to stay in shape. In other words, I did a complete makeover of my lifestyle.

Maybe at this point I should have had a clear sense of my readers in mind.

But I didn't really consider who my readers might be. There was no need to. I was in my early thirties then, and it was obvious my readers were the same age as me or perhaps younger. Young men and women, in other words. At the time I was considered a "rising young writer" (I'm a little embarrassed to use the term), and the people who supported my work were clearly the younger generation of readers. And what kind of people they were, and what they thought about, was not something I had to ponder much. My readers and myself as a writer were, as a matter of course, one. It was a sort of honeymoon period, I suppose, between me and my readers.

As I recall, for a number of reasons *A Wild Sheep Chase* got a cool reception from the editorial staff at the magazine *Gunzo*, which first published it, but fortunately many readers enjoyed it, reviews were positive, and it sold more than expected. In short, it was a smooth start for me as a professional, full-time writer. And I got the strong sense that I was moving in the right direction. In that way, *A Wild Sheep Chase* was my real starting point as a novelist.

TIME HAS PASSED. I am now far removed from being a rising young writer. I didn't plan it, but as time passes you naturally age (not much you can do about it). And as time has passed, of course the kind of readers who read my books has also changed. But if I were asked what kind of people read my books now I'd have to say I have no idea. I really don't.

I get a lot of letters from readers, and have the opportunities sometimes to actually meet some of them. But there's nothing connecting their ages, sex, and places they live, so I really have no mental picture of the main type of people who read my books. I get the feeling the sales departments at the publishers don't have a good grasp of it, either. My readers are about evenly split between men and women, and apart from the fact that many of my women readers are quite beautiful—this is no lie—there's no characteristic that they all share. In the past it seemed one trend was that I sold well in urban areas but not so much outside, but now there doesn't seem to be any clear regional difference.

I can imagine people might ask, "Are you saying you write your novels with no idea who your readers are?" Well, come to think of it, that's absolutely right. I have no clear mental image of my readership.

As far as I know, most writers age along with their readers. What I mean is that a writer's readers generally age in tandem with him. So in many cases the writer's age and the readers' ages overlap. Easy enough to understand. If that's the case, then you write novels assuming that your readers are the same age as you. But for me that doesn't seem to be true.

There are genres, of course, that target a predetermined age group or audience. Young-adult fiction, for instance, targets teenage boys and girls, romance fiction is written for women in their twenties and thirties, while historical novels and period fiction mainly targets middle-aged and older men. Again, easy to understand. But the novels I write seem a bit different.

Which takes us all the way around, back to where I began. Since

I have no idea what kind of people read my novels, all I can do is write them so I myself enjoy them. Back to the starting point, you might say, which is kind of strange.

Since I became a writer, though, and started regularly publishing books, there is one lesson I've learned. Which is that no matter what or how I write, somebody's going to say something bad about it. Say I write a really long novel, someone is bound to say, "It's too long. Too verbose. Half that length would be fine." If I write a short novel, some complain that it's too "shallow," too "hollow," that I'm "just phoning it in." If I write a novel similar to an earlier one, they say, "He's just repeating himself. He's stuck in a groove and it's boring." And others will say, "His earlier work was better. This new approach is just going round and round and getting nowhere." Come to think of it, for the last twenty-five years there have been people who say, "Murakami's out of step with the times. He's finished." It's easy to criticize—all you have to do is say what you're thinking, and you don't have to take any responsibility for anything. For the person who's being criticized, though, if he takes each and every criticism seriously he'll never survive. So I've concluded, "Whatever. If people are going to say terrible things, then I'm just going to write what I want to write, in the way I want to write it."

Rick Nelson had a song late in his career called "Garden Party." The lyrics included the following:

See, you can't please everyone
So you got to please yourself.

I know exactly how he feels. It's impossible to please everyone, and all you end up doing is spinning your wheels and wearing yourself out. In that case it's better to stand up for yourself and do what makes you happy, what you really want to do, the way you want to do it. Do that, and even if your reputation isn't so great, if your books don't sell well, you can tell yourself, "It's okay. At least I enjoyed myself." You'll be convinced it was all worthwhile.

Thelonious Monk said something apropos of this: "I say, play your own way. Don't play what the public wants. You play what you want and let the public pick up on what you're doing—even if it does take them fifteen, twenty years."

Enjoying yourself doesn't necessarily mean you'll produce an outstanding work of art. A process of rigorous self-examination is a crucial element. Also, as a professional, of course you need a minimum number of readers. But clear that hurdle and I think that your goal should be to enjoy yourself and write works that satisfy you. I mean, a life spent doing something you don't find enjoyable can't be much fun, right? I return again to our starting point: What's wrong about feeling good?

S T I L L , if someone asks me straight up, "Do you mean to tell me you really write novels only thinking about yourself?" I'd have to respond that of course that's not the case. As I've said before, as a professional writer I always have readers in mind as I write. Forgetting about the existence of readers—if you wanted to—is impossible, and is also not a healthy thing to do.

But saying I keep readers in mind isn't the same as a company, when it's developing a new product, surveying the market, analyzing consumers, and zeroing in on a target audience. What always comes to my mind is more an "imaginary reader." That person doesn't have an age, an occupation, or a gender. In reality he would, but those are interchangeable in my mind. In other words they're not important elements. What is important, what is not interchangeable, is the fact that that person and I are connected. I don't know the details of where and how we're connected. Yet I get the distinct sense that deep down, in some dark recesses, my roots and that person's roots are linked. It's such a deep, dark place, not something you can casually drop by and see. Yet through the system of narrative, I feel that we are connected, the real sense that nourishment is passing back and forth.

Yet if that person and I were to pass each other in some back street, or be seated next to each other on a train, or lined up together at the same checkout counter in a supermarket, we wouldn't (in most cases) notice that our roots are connected in that way. We'd just pass by each other, strangers, and go our separate ways without ever realizing it. Probably never to see each other again. But *in reality*, down deep in the ground, in a place that penetrates below the hard crust of everyday life, we are, novelistically, connected. Deep within our hearts we share a common narrative. That's probably the type of reader I assume. And every day I write my novels with the hope that that reader will enjoy them a little, and feel something when he reads them.

Compared to that, the actual people around me in everyday life can be a lot of trouble. Every time I write a new book some people like it, and others don't. Even if they don't clearly express their opinions and thoughts, I can usually read it in their faces. It's only to be expected. Everybody has preferences. I can work as hard as I want, but as Rick Nelson said, you can't please everyone. Seeing everybody's individual reactions is, for the writer, pretty exhausting. Those are the times I simply take a stand and say, "You got to please yourself." I'm able to keep these two stances distinct, which is a skill I've learned over long years of writing. Maybe it's the wisdom I need in order to live.

ONE THING that makes me very happy is that people of many different age groups seem to be reading my novels. I often get letters to the effect that "all three generations in my home are reading your works, Mr. Murakami." The grandmother is reading them (perhaps one of my "young readers" from years past), the mother's reading them, and so is her son and his younger sister . . . This kind of scenario seems pretty common. Hearing that really cheers me up. A copy of one book being passed around to several people in a family means that book really has a life of its own. Of course if each one bought their own copy, that would boost sales and make the publisher happy; but as the author of the book, honestly, I'm far happier if five people cherish the one copy.

Which reminds me of a phone call I got once from a former classmate. "My son, who's in high school, has read all your books," he told me, "and we often talk together about them. We normally don't talk too much, but when it comes to your books we're able to say a lot to each other." He sounded happy when he said this. "Oh," I thought, "so my books *do* have a small role to play in the world." At least to help a parent and child communicate. That's an achievement. I don't have children myself, and if other people's children enjoy reading my books, and that arouses a response in them, that means I've passed on something to the next generation, albeit in a modest way.

Realistically speaking, though, I have hardly any individual, direct relations with any of my readers. In Japan, I don't make public appearances, first of all, and rarely appear before the media. I've never been on TV or radio, even once (though I've been caught on film a few times against my wishes).* I don't do public book signings. People ask me why, and the reason is I'm a professional writer, what I can do best is write novels, and as much as I can I want to invest all my energy in that. Life is short, and I have only so much time and energy. I don't want to use up time in something apart from my main occupation. Abroad, though, I do a public talk, a reading, or a book signing about once a year. I see this as my duty as a Japanese writer, something I have to do on occasion. I'll delve into that topic more some other time.

I have, though, set up websites a few times. They were only online for a few weeks at a time, but I received countless emails from readers. And I made it a rule to look at each and every one. I might skim through the really long ones, but I did read every email sent to me.

And I wrote a reply to about one out of every ten. I would answer questions, give a bit of advice, give my reaction to the message, etc. The exchanges were of all sorts, from casual comments to fairly serious, formal replies. During that time (which might extend over several months) I work like mad to reply to the emails, hardly taking on any other work; yet it seems like most people who get a reply from me don't believe I actually wrote it myself. They think someone else wrote it for me. There are many cases where replies to fan letters to celebrities are written by others hired for the job, so they must think I do the same. I made it clear on these websites that all replies are written directly by me, but it seems like most of the time people don't take that at face value.

I hear that especially with young women: they'll be really happy

---

* Editor's Note: After the original publication of this book, Haruki Murakami began hosting his own radio program, *Murakami Radio*, in Japan.

telling their boyfriend, "I got a reply from Haruki Murakami himself!" and their boyfriend will often put a damper on that, telling them, "Don't be stupid. Murakami's too busy to write each reply himself. He has someone else write them for him, and just says he writes them himself." There really are a lot of suspicious people in the world, apparently (or maybe it's that there are a lot of people who try to deceive others). But the truth is, I work very hard to answer these myself. I think I'm pretty fast at writing replies, but with the great number of emails I get, it's a lot of work, believe me. But it is fun to do it, and I learn a lot.

And through that exchange of emails with actual readers, I've come to understand something: as a whole, people have a really solid grasp of my work. Sometimes I'll find misinterpretations, or places where they're overthinking things, and occasionally emails where (pardon me for saying so) I think they've got things a bit mixed up. Even my self-styled *fervent fans* will, depending on the work, like some and be critical of others. Some works they'll respond to, others they'll resist. The opinions I hear from them are all over the place. But when I take a step back and look at the whole picture they paint from a distance, I get the distinct sense that my readers really read my works deeply, and understand what they're all about. There are small, differences, depending on the person, some of whom are more on target than others, but if you deduct those and average it all out, in the final analysis they wind up where they should be.

"Ah!" I think when I read them. "So that's how they see it?" Like mist clearing up over a ridge. Gaining this awareness was, for me, a rare and valuable experience. An Internet experience, I guess you'd say. Though it was such hard work I doubt I'll be able to do it again.

I mentioned having an "imaginary reader" in mind when I write, and I think the definition is almost the same as this image of a "whole readership." But since the image of a "whole" is too broad to get a mental picture of, I've compressed it into a single entity and called it an "imaginary reader."

IN BOOKSTORES IN JAPAN, male writers' and female writers' works are often placed in separate corners, something you don't see in bookstores abroad. Maybe there are some, but at least I've never seen them divided this way. I've given some thought to why they divide things like this, and came to the conclusion that perhaps women readers read more books by female writers while men readers read books by male writers. So it's a question of convenience, placing the two groups in separate areas in a bookstore to make it easier for readers. When I think of my own reading habits, I realize I tend to read a few more books by male writers than by women writers, too, though not because I decide from the start I'll read something just because it's by a man. It just turns out that way. Of course there are a lot of women writers I enjoy. Among foreign writers I love Jane Austen and Carson McCullers. I've read all their books. I like Alice Munro, too, and I've translated several of Grace Paley's works. So I get the feeling it's wrong to have male and female writers' works plunked down in separate areas of a bookstore. It's just going to make the division of which works are read by which sex even more pronounced. Not that society's going to listen to what I have to say about it.

As I mentioned a little earlier, readers of my works seem about equally divided between men and women. I haven't compiled statistics to back this up, but through meeting and talking with readers, and through the email exchange I mentioned, I get the sense that my readers are about equally male and female. It's true of Japan, and also seems true abroad. There's a nice balance. I don't know why it's this way, but I get the feeling it's something I should be genuinely pleased about. The world's population is about half men and half women, so it's a natural and healthy thing for my readers to be evenly split as well.

Once when I was talking with a young woman reader, she asked me, "Mr. Murakami, how is it that though you're a man in your sixties, you understand young women's feelings so well?" (Naturally, there are lots of people who don't share this opinion; I'm just giving this as the opinion one reader had.) I've never thought that I have a good handle on young women's feelings, so (truly) I was quite surprised to hear this. I would probably respond with something like, "As I write a story, I try very hard to put myself inside the characters, and gradually I might get a sense of what they're feeling or thinking. But always just in a novelistic sense."

In other words, as I move the characters around in the framework of the novel I get to understand these to a degree, but this is a bit different from understanding real-life young women. Unfortunately, I should say, when it comes to flesh-and-blood people, I don't understand them so well. But still, knowing that flesh-and-blood young women—at least a certain segment of them—enjoy reading the novels I (an old guy in his mid-sixties) have written, and can feel sympathy for the characters that appear in them, makes me happier than anything. It almost feels miraculous.

I'm certainly not against there being books targeting male readers and others targeting female readers. Those kinds of books are definitely needed. But I hope that the books I write will arouse and move readers in the same way regardless of sex. And if lovers, groups of men and women, or married couples, children and parents, enthusiastically discuss my books together, nothing could please me more. I have always believed that novels, and stories, function to allay and blunt the sharp edges of all kinds of stereotypical sources of friction—friction between men and women, between the generations. Needless to say, that's a wonderful function. I have a quiet hope that the novels I write can take on this sort of positive role, even a little, in our world.

I N A W O R D —though it sounds a bit clichéd, and I hesitate to say it—I feel very strongly that ever since I debuted as a writer I've been blessed with readers. I seem to be repeating myself, but critically I was put in a difficult position for many years. Even within the publishing companies who published my books, there were often more editors who were critical of my work than those who supported it. Because of that I was always hearing critical comments and was treated coldly. It seems like all I've done is quietly kept on working, all by myself, despite the strong headwinds blowing against me (though there have been variations over time in their intensity).

Even so, I've been able to soldier on without getting disheartened or depressed (though I admit to times when I feel worn out), because readers have stayed with my works. Again, perhaps I'm not the one to say this, but these are high-quality readers. They don't just say, finishing the book, "That was interesting" and toss it aside and forget about it; the majority of them ask themselves *why* they found it interesting, and go on to consider it all over again. And some of my readers—a not inconsiderable number—go on to reread the book. In some cases, they read it many times over several decades. Some will lend the book to close friends to get them to read it, and then discuss their opinions and impressions of the book together. Through all sorts of ways, then, they get a fuller understanding of the book and can corroborate their response to it. Countless readers have told me this. And each time I feel a deep sense of gratitude. Because for an author this is exactly the way the ideal type of reader should be. (That's the way I used to read books myself, too, back when I was young.)

And another thing I feel a little proud of is that as I've published books over the last thirty-five years, the number of readers has steadily climbed. *Norwegian Wood*, of course, sold the most by far; but apart from that *floating layer* of readers and the temporary surge in numbers, it appears that the numbers of the *base layer*— those who wait for my latest book and buy it and read it—have continuously, and steadily, gone up. You can see that in the numbers, but I also get a strong visceral sense of it myself, too. Again, this is happening not just in Japan but overseas as well. Interestingly, readers both in Japan and abroad understand my books in pretty much the same way.

To put it another way, over a long period of time I think I've constructed a system whereby readers and myself are connected by a stout pipeline that allows us to communicate. This is a system in which the media and the literary industry aren't needed much as an intermediary. What's needed most there is a natural, spontaneous *sense of trust* between author and readers. Without a feeling of trust, in which many readers feel "If it's one of Murakami's books, then I'll buy it and read it, and I know I won't regret it"—without this sense of trust, no matter how thick this direct pipeline may be, the system won't stand for long.

Years ago, I happened to meet and talk with the author John

Irving, and he told me an interesting thing about his connections with readers. "The most important thing," he said, "is to mainline the readers. I know it's kind of a coarse way of putting it." To create this unbreakable connection between you where the reader can't wait for the next hit. I get it as a metaphor, but since the image is so antisocial I prefer using the gentler expression "direct pipeline." But what we're saying is nearly the same. You have to have that kind of intimate, physical sensation—that "Hey, bro, got something here you're gonna love" sense—that sort of direct deal between author and reader.

I sometimes get interesting letters from readers. "I read your latest book, Mr. Murakami, and was disappointed. Unfortunately I just couldn't get into it. But I'm definitely buying the next one. Keep up the good work!" That kind of message. Truth be told, I love readers like that and am very grateful for them. Because in that message there's a clear *sense of trust*. And that makes me feel I'd better do a great job on the next book. And I hope with all my heart that he/she will like it. Of course, since "you can't please everyone," I don't know if it will actually turn out that way or not.

Going Abroad: A New Frontier

↳

M Y W O R K S were first really introduced in America near the end of the 1980s. This happened when Kodansha International (KI), a subsidiary of the Japanese publisher Kodansha, published a hardcover edition of the English translation of my novel *A Wild Sheep Chase*, and several of my short stories were published in *The New Yorker*. At the time Kodansha International had an office in central Manhattan, hired local editors on staff, and was very actively promoting Japanese literature. They were attempting to venture into the American publishing industry. Later on, this company became Kodansha America (KA).

Elmer Luke, a Chinese American man, led the editorial team, and there were several other able staff members as well, specialists in PR and sales. The president was a Mr. Tetsu Shirai, the type who didn't insist on running the company in a typically fussy Japanese style but let the American staff work as they pleased. So the atmosphere at the company was pretty relaxed. The American staff there were very enthusiastic about getting my work published in the US. Later on, I lived in New Jersey, so when I went into New York I'd stop by the KA office on Broadway and enjoy talking with them. The atmosphere was more like a US company than a Japanese one. The staff were all New Yorkers, very lively and capable, and it was a real pleasure working with them. I have a lot of good memories from those times. I was almost forty at the time, and all kinds of interesting things happened in my life then. Even now I keep in touch with some of these staff members.

Thanks to Alfred Birnbaum's lively translation, *A Wild Sheep Chase* was better received than expected, reviewed at length in *The New York Times* and praised by John Updike in a review in *The New Yorker*. In terms of sales, though, it wasn't all that successful. Kodansha International was still a newcomer in the publishing world, and I was of course unknown, and books like that aren't displayed very prominently in bookstores. It might have been better if they'd had e-books and online shopping like now, but back then these were still a long way off. So though the book did get talked about, this didn't translate directly into sales. Later, though, when *A Wild Sheep Chase* came out in a Vintage paperback edition, it turned into a book with strong and steady sales.

We next published *Hard-Boiled Wonderland and the End of the World* and *Dance Dance Dance*, and these were also well reviewed and got noticed, but they were seen more as books for a niche readership, and again sales could have been better. At the time Japan's economy was roaring, a go-go time when one bestseller was titled *Japan as Number One;* but cultural influences from Japan were minimal. When I talked with Americans, the topic usually centered on economic issues, and no one seemed interested in cultural topics. Ryuichi Sakamoto and Banana Yoshimoto were getting known at the time (even more so in Europe), though in the US market at least they weren't enough to create a trend that got people to pay attention to Japanese culture. To put it bluntly, Japan was seen as a country "rolling in wealth but basically mysterious." Naturally there were those who read Kawabata, Tanizaki, and Mishima, and prized Japanese literature, but these were just a handful of intellectuals. For the most part your more discerning urban readers.

So I was overjoyed when several of my short stories sold to *The New Yorker* (as a longtime fan of the magazine, it was like a dream to get my work published in it), but unfortunately I couldn't break out to the next level. If you liken it to a rocket, it's like the takeoff was fine but the second-stage booster didn't work. But still, my close relationship with *The New Yorker* has continued up to the present day, through changes in the editors and literary editors, with the magazine becoming a reassuring home ground for me in America. The editors there seem genuinely fond of my style (which maybe suits their magazine's image), and we made an exclusive writer's contract. I felt quite honored when I later discovered that they'd made the same kind of contract with J. D. Salinger.

In the twenty-five years since my first short story was published in *The New Yorker* ("TV People," September 10, 1990) and the timing of this writing, in 2015, I've had twenty-seven stories accepted and published in the magazine. The editorial department is very strict about choosing which stories to accept and which to reject, and they reject (it's said) any work that doesn't meet their set standards and tastes, no matter how famous the writer might be and how close his relationship might be to the editorial staff. The staff even unanimously turned down Salinger's story "Zooey," though ultimately it was published in the magazine through the efforts of the editor at the time, William Shawn. Of course I've had many works rejected. This makes it very different from magazines in Japan. But passing through this tough selection process and having my works regularly featured in *The New Yorker* has really helped me develop a readership in the US and gradually get my name known more widely. Its role has been crucial in my career abroad.

It's hard for magazines in Japan to imagine the level of prestige and influence *The New Yorker* wields. Tell people in America that your novel sold a million copies in Japan or won some literary prize and they're basically unimpressed, but get published in *The New Yorker* and they start treating you very differently. I often find myself envious of a culture like this, where such a landmark magazine exists.

SEVERAL AMERICANS I met through my work cautioned me, saying, "It's difficult to be successful as a writer in America unless you sign a contract with a US agent and have your books come out from one of the major publishers." And it goes without saying that I felt the same way. At least that was the situation back at the time. I felt bad toward the people at KA, but I decided to go out on my own and find an agent and a new publisher.

After interviewing several people in New York, I decided to work with Amanda "Binky" Urban at the major agency ICM (International Creative Management); with the publisher Alfred A. Knopf (an imprint of what was then Random House) and its president and editor-in-chief, Sonny Mehta; and with the editor Gary Fisketjon. All three, at the time, were leading figures in the literary world in the US. Looking back at it now, I'm surprised how people of their caliber showed an interest in me, but I was desperate then and gave little thought to how important these people were. I just went with connections acquaintances of mine had, talked with a lot of people, and picked the ones I thought would be best.

I think there were three reasons why these three were interested in me. One is that I was a translator of Raymond Carver's work and was the person who introduced him into Japan. The three of them were, in order, Raymond Carver's agent, his publisher, and his chief editor. I don't see this as mere coincidence. Perhaps the late Ray Carver was leading me to them. (At the time it was still just four or five years after he had passed away.)

The second reason was that my novel *Norwegian Wood* had, as a two-volume set, sold two million copies in Japan, something that got into the news even in the US. Even in America literary works rarely sell two million copies. Thanks to this, my name started to get known in the US publishing world, with *Norwegian Wood* my calling card of sorts.

The third reason was that I had started to steadily publish works in the US, which people had begun to notice, and I was seen as a *promising* newcomer. The fact that *The New Yorker* thought highly of me was a tremendous influence. The legendary editor of *The New Yorker*, Robert Gottlieb, who succeeded William Shawn, for some reason took a personal liking to me, and I have a wonderful memory of him personally giving me a tour around the offices of the magazine. The literary editor I worked with directly, Linda Asher, was a charming woman, and got along amazingly well with me. She stepped down a long time ago from *The New Yorker*, but we're still close. Looking back on it, it's like *The New Yorker* trained me for the US market.

The result was that getting connected with these three people in the publishing world (Binky Urban, Sonny Mehta, and Gary Fisketjon) was a major reason that things went well. They were all very talented, enthusiastic people, with numerous contacts and a decided amount of influence in publishing. One other thing is that from my early collection *The Elephant Vanishes* to my latest novel, the covers of my books were all designed by Chip Kidd, the well-known designer for Knopf, and were all well received. There are people who wait for my new books just because they're looking forward to his cover designs. Having Chip work on my books was another great blessing. (Author's note: Sonny passed away in 2019, and Gary retired from Knopf in the same year. Binky and I are still working together.)

And another reason I was successful, I believe, was that though I was technically a Japanese writer, I put that aside and was, from the very first, determined to stand on a level playing field with other American authors. I found my own translators and had them translate the works for me personally, checked them myself, then brought the translated manuscripts to my agent to sell to the publisher. This way my agent and publisher treated me the same way they would an American writer. Not as a foreign writer writing novels in a foreign language, but as someone standing on the same playing field as American novelists, playing by the same rules. The first thing I did was to make sure this system was firmly in place.

I decided this the first time I met Binky and she told me, in no uncertain terms, that she doesn't deal with works she can't read in English. She reads works herself, determines their value, and only then starts to work on getting them published. So if you bring in books she can't read, you won't get anywhere. It's only natural, I suppose, for a literary agent. That's why I made sure, at the time, to have satisfactory English translations ready.

People in publishing in Japan and Europe often say American publishers are commercialized, only concerned about sales, and don't take the time needed to develop writers. It doesn't rise to the level of being anti-American, but I often feel an antipathy (or lack of goodwill) toward the American-style business model. It would be a lie to say that the American publishing industry is totally free of that aspect. I've met several US writers who've told me, "Agents and publishers are wonderful to you when you're selling well, but if you don't sell, then they give you the cold shoulder." I do believe that does happen. But that's not all there is to it. I've seen examples where for a certain work they're fond of, or an author they think is *the one*, agents and publishers will concentrate on developing them without worrying about the short-term bottom line. Here an editor's personal devotion and enthusiasm for a work plays a key role. I think this must be about the same anywhere in the world.

As far as I can see, in any country people who go into the publishing field or want to become editors basically love books. Even in America, if someone wants to earn a lot and have a huge expense account, they don't go into publishing. They either work on Wall Street or on Madison Avenue. Other than a few rare exceptions, salaries in the publishing industry aren't that high. So the people who work there, for the most part, have the pride and spirit that come from knowing they are doing it because they truly love books. Once they love a book, they work hard to promote it, but not because they're concerned about sales.

Since I lived on the East Coast of the US for a time (New Jersey and Boston), I got to develop a close personal relationship with Binky, Sonny, and Gary. I live far away now, but when I was nearby or visiting, I tried to get together every once in a while to talk and have a meal together. This applies in any country, I think. If you let your agent handle everything and never meet the people involved, thinking you'll leave it all up to them, then nothing will ever get going. Naturally, if you're talking about an immensely powerful literary work, then those things aren't so necessary; but truthfully, I wasn't that confident, and I'm the type who, in anything, likes to do whatever I can do myself, so that's what I did. What I did when I debuted in Japan I did all over again in America. In my forties I pushed the reset button back to being a *newcomer*.

I ACTIVELY SET OUT to develop a market in the US like this because all sorts of unpleasant things had happened back in Japan, and I felt that I couldn't just sit around idly in Japan, content with the status quo. This was during Japan's so-called bubble economy, and back then making a living as a writer wasn't all that difficult. First of all, there's a pretty large readership base (the population is over one hundred million, nearly all of whom read Japanese). On top of this the Japanese economy was booming globally, and business in the publishing industry was brisk. The stock market was booming, land prices were soaring, and there was a glut of money, and new magazines appeared one after the other and were able to get as much advertising as they wanted to. Writers had no trouble getting requests for work. At the time, I got any number of tempting offers. "Travel wherever you want in the world," I was told once, "all expenses paid, and write any kind of travel essay you wish." Once a person I didn't even know made a tantalizing offer: "I just bought a chateau in France, so why don't you live there for a year and enjoy writing a novel there?" (I politely declined both offers.) It's hard to believe now that such a time ever existed. For novelists, even if their staple work, novels, didn't sell that well, they could make a good living on all these "side dishes."

But for me, on the cusp of forty (a critical time for a writer), this wasn't a welcome situation. There's an expression, "The hearts of the people are chaotic," and that was exactly the situation then. Society as a whole was uncertain, with people basically just concerned about money. It wasn't the type of atmosphere where I could concentrate and take the time to work on a lengthy novel. I got the strong sense that before I knew it, I'd get completely spoiled. I wanted to put myself in an edgier environment and carve out a new frontier. And try out new possibilities for myself. That's how I was thinking, and why, in the late 1980s, I left Japan and lived mainly abroad. This was after I had published *Hard-Boiled Wonderland and the End of the World*.

ONE OTHER THING is that in Japan, my books—and often me personally—were sometimes severely criticized. My basic attitude is that I'm an imperfect person writing imperfect works, so it doesn't matter what people say, and I haven't worried much about others' opinions; but at the time I was still young, and when I heard these criticisms they often struck me as totally unfair. Criticism even ventured into my private life, my family, with things written that were totally untrue, and some personal attacks as well. "Why do people have to say those kinds of things?" I wondered, finding it all more puzzling than unpleasant.

Looking back on it now, I get the feeling this was the Japanese literary world (writers, critics, editors, etc.) at the time venting its frustration. The result of the discontent and gloominess inside the *literary industry* toward the rapid decline in the presence and influence of the so-called mainstream (pure literature). In other words, a gradual paradigm shift was taking place. People in publishing, though, found this cultural meltdown lamentable and they couldn't stand it. Many of them thought of my works, and my *very existence,* as "one of the causes that has hurt and destroyed the way things should be" and, like white blood cells attacking a virus, tried to drive me out. That's the feeling I got. For my part, I felt that if the likes of me could damage them, then the problem lay more with them than with me.

"Haruki Murakami's works are merely a rehash of foreign literature," I often hear. "The only place they'll be read in is Japan." I never ever thought of what I write as "a rehash of foreign literature"; rather, it was an attempt to use the tools of Japanese to actively seek and search for new possibilities—so to tell the truth I saw these remarks as a challenge, that whether my works were read and appreciated abroad would be a kind of test. I'm not really the type of personality who hates to lose, but when I'm not convinced by something I do tend to pursue it until I am.

Also, if my work is centered more on foreign countries, then there will be less of a need to deal with the troublesome domestic literary industry. Then they can say what they want and I can just ignore it. This possibility was another reason I decided to focus on doing my best abroad. If you think about it, since criticism within Japan was the opportunity for me to start up activities abroad, you might conversely say I was lucky to be disparaged in that way. It's the same in every world, but nothing's more scary than a back-handed compliment.

The thing that made me happiest when I published my books abroad was how many people (both readers and critics) said my books were really "original," unlike anything by any other novelists. Whether they praised the works or not, the basic consensus was that "this writer's style is totally unlike any other's." This assessment was quite different from that in Japan, and it made me very happy. To say that I was original, that I had my own special style—for me nothing could be higher praise.

But when my books started to sell abroad—or I should say when they found out my books were selling abroad—now people in Japan started saying, "Murakami's books sell abroad because they're written in easy-to-translate language, about things foreigners can easily understand." When I heard this I was a bit disgusted. "Isn't this the exact opposite of what you were saying before?" But I figured there was nothing I could do about it. All I could conclude was that there are a certain number of people in the world who check which way the wind's blowing and make casual, completely unfounded remarks.

Novels well up naturally from within you, not something you can casually, strategically change. You can't do market research or something and then intentionally rework the content based on the results. If you did, a work born from such a shallow base won't find many readers. Such a work might find a readership for a time, but the work and the author won't last long and will soon be forgotten. Abraham Lincoln's famous saying "You can fool all the people some of the time, and some of the people all the time, but you cannot fool all the people all the time" can apply to novels, too. There are a lot of things in this world that are demonstrated over time that can only be demonstrated over time.

LET ME GET BACK ON TOPIC.

Knopf published hardcover editions of my novels, and its paperback imprint, Vintage Books, published the paperback editions; and over time, as a series of my books appeared, sales in the US gradually but steadily increased. When a new novel was published, it would land near the top of bestseller lists in newspapers in cities like Boston and San Francisco. A readership base developed in the US, just as it had in Japan—people who were sure to buy my new books whenever they appeared.

And after about 2000, my books, such as *Kafka on the Shore* (published in the US in 2005), started to appear, though near the bottom, as national bestsellers on *The New York Times* bestseller list. Which meant that around the country, my novelistic style was becoming appreciated. *1Q84* (published in 2011) made number 2 on the bestseller list, while *Colorless Tsukuru Tazaki and His Years of Pilgrimage* (2014) debuted at number 1. But getting to this point took a long time. I wasn't an overnight sensation. Instead, it felt like I finally established a foothold as one book steadily followed another. As this happened, sales of the paperback editions of my earlier books picked up, too. Which was definitely a favorable trend.

IN THE EARLY STAGES, though, what stood out was less what was happening in the US than the increase in the number of copies of my books printed in Europe. Making New

York the hub for overseas publishing seemed to have an influence on sales in Europe, a development I hadn't foreseen. Truthfully, up till then I hadn't realized that it was that important to have a hub based in New York. I'd simply made the US my temporary home, figuring that if the books are in English people will read them, and because I happened to live in the US.

Aside from Asia, the first place my books really took off was in Russia and Eastern Europe, and my impression is that this then spread into Western Europe. This was the middle of the 1990s. I was really surprised when I heard that about half of the top ten bestselling books in Russia at one time were mine.

This is just my personal impression, and I'd be hard pressed to give any proof or examples to back it up, but I get the feeling that if you compare sales of my books with a historical timeline there's a tendency worldwide for my books to start being read widely after there is a major shake-up (or transformation) in the social foundations of a country. My books started selling rapidly in Russia and Eastern Europe after the seismic shift when communism collapsed. The heretofore seemingly solid, unshakable communist system collapsed overnight to be followed by a steadily surging *soft chaos*, a mix of hope and anxiety. In the midst of that shift in values, the stories I presented suddenly seemed tinged with a new, natural reality.

The wall separating East and West Berlin dramatically came down, and from around the time of German reunification, it seems like my books gradually started to be read more in Germany. Maybe it's just a coincidence. But it seems to me that a huge transformation in the foundations and structure of a society has a profound influence on people's everyday sense of reality, and the desire for transformation is only to be expected. The reality of actual society and the reality of stories are inevitably connected at a fundamental level in people's souls (or in their unconscious). In any age, when something major occurs and there's a shift in social reality, there's a related yearning for a shift in the reality of stories as well.

Stories can exist as metaphors for reality, and people need to internalize new stories (and new systems of metaphor) in order to cope with an unfolding new reality. By successfully connecting these two systems, the system of actual society and the metaphoric system—by, to put it another way, allowing movement between the objective world and the subjective world so they mutually modify each other—people are able to accept an uncertain reality and maintain their sanity. I get the sense that the reality in the stories I provide in my fiction just happens to function globally as a kind of cogwheel that makes that adjustment possible. Naturally, this is, to repeat myself, just my own individual sense of things. But I don't think it's entirely off the mark.

In that sense, Japanese society may have—at an earlier stage and as something more self-evidently understood—observed that overall landslide in a more natural, less dramatic fashion. It follows that my novels were more enthusiastically accepted in Japan—at least among ordinary readers—than in the West. The same thing might be said about the neighboring countries in East Asia—China, Korea, and Taiwan. Readers in these countries started enthusiastically appreciating my works before they were accepted in America and Europe.

It's possible that this societal landslide had a reality for people in these East Asian countries before it did for people in Europe and the US. And this wasn't the sort of sudden social transformation that occurred because of some particular events, but a softer landslide over time. In other words, in the Asian countries that went through rapid economic growth the social landslide wasn't some sudden occurrence but, rather, a constant, sustained situation taking place over the last quarter of a century.

I know it's a bit forced to make a simple assertion like this, since there are all sorts of other causes involved. But certainly there is a perceptible discrepancy in the reactions of readers to my novels in various Asian countries and the reactions of readers in Europe and the US. And I think in great part this comes down to differences in the way they perceived and coped with this landslide. For that matter, I get the sense that in Japan and Asian countries the "modern" that necessarily precedes the "postmodern" did not, in a precise sense, exist. The split between the subjective and the objective was never as logically clear there as in the West. But this takes us off in divergent directions, so I'll leave that discussion to another time.

ONE OTHER IMPORTANT REASON I was able to make a breakthrough in the West was that I was blessed with several outstanding translators. Around the middle of the 1980s a shy young American named Alfred Birnbaum came to see me, saying he'd loved my work and was translating a few of my short stories, and asked whether it was okay that he do so. "Sure," I replied. "Please go right ahead." He translated even more stories over time, and eventually this led to me being published in *The New Yorker*. Alfred went on to translate *A Wild Sheep Chase*, *Hard-Boiled Wonderland and the End of the World*, and *Dance Dance Dance* for Kodansha International. Alfred is an extremely talented, enthusiastic translator. If he hadn't come to me with that request,

I don't think I would have even thought at that point of having my works translated into English. I didn't think my works had reached that level yet.

Later on, I was invited to Princeton and started living in the US, and at this point I met Jay Rubin. He was a professor at the University of Washington then, and later taught at Harvard. An outstanding researcher in Japanese literature, he was known for his translations of several works by Natsume Sōseki. He was interested in my work, too, and asked me to contact him if I ever needed any of my works translated. "To start off with," I asked him, "would you mind translating a few of my short stories that you like?" He selected a few and translated them, and his translations were outstanding. What I found most interesting was that he and Alfred chose completely different stories. It was amazing how they didn't overlap in their choices. I keenly felt then how important it is to have several translators working on your fiction.

Jay Rubin is a very skilled translator, and I think his translation of *The Wind-Up Bird Chronicle* really helped establish me in the US. In a word, Alfred is a more freewheeling translator, while Jay is more the steady type. Each one has his own distinctive flavor, but at the time Alfred was busy with his own work and didn't have the time to work on long novels, so I was very happy that Jay appeared on the scene. I also think that a translator like Jay, who makes sure to get the accurate, literal meaning, was well suited to translating a novel like *The Wind-Up Bird Chronicle*, with its relatively intricate structure (compared to my earlier works). Another aspect of his translations I enjoy is his unaffected sense of humor. Not merely his accuracy and dependability.

Next come Philip Gabriel and Ted Goossen. They are both quite skilled translators, and both of them were quite interested in my work, too. I've known them both for a long time, since I was young. Each one approached me saying he'd like to translate my work or that he had already translated some. I felt very grateful for this. Meeting them, making a personal connection with them, made me feel like I'd made some invaluable allies. I myself am a translator (English into Japanese), so I well know from personal experience the struggles and joys of being a translator. So I try to keep in close touch with them and am always happy to answer any translation questions that might crop up. I do my best to make things more convenient for them.

If you try it yourself, you'll discover that translating is painstaking, arduous work. But it shouldn't be a one-sided undertaking. There's got to be an element of give-and-take involved. For a writer wanting to be read abroad, a translator is the most important partner of all. It's critical to find a translator who understands you, because even with an outstanding translator, if he isn't on the same wavelength as the text or the author, or can't get used to the distinct qualities of the work, you can't expect any good results. All you'll get is both sides stressed out. And if the translator has no affection for the text he's working on, it'll just be an irksome "job" he has to slog through.

THERE'S ONE MORE THING—maybe something I don't need to actually put into words—but abroad, especially in the West, the individual is paramount. You can't act the way you do in Japan, and just let somebody else handle things and tell them "Thanks for taking care of everything." At each step of the way you have to take responsibility and make decisions yourself. This takes time and effort, as well as a certain linguistic ability. Literary agents, of course, will take care of all the basics, but they can be busy with other work, and to tell the truth they can't get around to doing enough for unknown writers or ones who don't sell well. So to a certain extent you have to take care of things yourself. I'm pretty well-known in Japan, but abroad at first I was an unknown. Except for people in publishing and a handful of readers, ordinary people in America didn't know my name, and couldn't even pronounce it right, often mispronouncing it as "*Myu*rakami." But that only motivated me all the more. I put everything I had into it, really wanting to see how much I could open up a market starting from a blank slate.

As I said earlier, if I'd stayed in Japan, where times were good, as the bestselling author (if I can put it that way myself) of *Norwegian Wood*, I would have had one request after another and could have, if I'd wanted to, made a lot of money. But I wanted to leave that environment and, as an (almost) unknown writer, see how far I could go as a newcomer in the market outside Japan. That became my personal goal. And looking back on it now, I think having that goal as a kind of slogan was a great thing. It's important for those who deal with creativity to always want to push forward into new frontiers. Being content with where you are and staying in one place ("place" in a metaphoric sense) means your creative urge will atrophy and eventually be lost. I may have, at exactly the right time, found a worthy goal and a healthy sense of ambition.

Temperamentally I'm not good at being in front of other people, but abroad I have done interviews, and when I win an award I attend the ceremony and give a speech. I also have accepted a few opportunities to give readings and speeches. Not that many—even abroad I have the reputation of being a writer who doesn't make many personal appearances—but I do what I can, pushing the limits of my personal boundaries and being more open to the outside. I'm not that good at speaking English, but I try to speak without an interpreter as much as I can and give my opinions in my own words. In Japan, though, with rare exceptions, I don't do those things. And I get criticized for it, people saying I only provide this kind of service abroad, that I'm following a double standard.

I'm not saying this to justify myself, but the reason I try to appear in front of people more abroad is because I feel I have a duty as a Japanese writer that I need to fully accept. As I mentioned before, when I lived abroad during the bubble-economy period, I found it sad and dreary sometimes that Japanese were seen as "faceless." And the more I experienced that, I began to think that—for the many Japanese living abroad, and for myself, too—I needed to do my part to change that a little. I'm not a particularly patriotic type (I see myself as having more cosmopolitan tendencies), but like it or not, living abroad I became more conscious of myself as a *Japanese writer*. Others around me saw me this way, and I saw myself that way, too. And without knowing it, I developed a sense of fellowship with my countrymen. If you think about it, it's kind of strange. I escape from the land of Japan, from the rigid framework of its society, and live abroad as an expatriate, only to find myself compelled to return to a relationship with that very land.

To clarify, it's a not a return to the *land itself* but a return to a *relationship* with that land. There's a big difference. Sometimes I'll see people who come back from living abroad turning oddly patriotic (in some cases even ultranationalistic) as a kind of backlash, perhaps, but that's not true in my case. I just came to consider more deeply the meaning of my being a Japanese writer, and the place of that identity.

M Y W O R K S have now been translated into over fifty different languages. I'm proud of this accomplishment, since it means that my books are appreciated in the context of many cultures. As a writer this makes me very happy, and also proud. This doesn't mean, though, that I see what I've done as "right," and I'm not going to claim that. Again, apples and oranges. Even now I'm still developing as a writer, with the scope, maybe, or potential, for growth still (nearly) unlimited.

So where, I ask myself, do you think that potential lies?

It's found inside me, I believe. First, I established myself as a writer within Japan, then turned my attention abroad, and widened the scope of my readership. And after this, I think, I will go even more deeply down inside myself, probing even further and deeper within. For me that's a new, unknown land, the final frontier.

I don't know if I can effectively open up that frontier, but as I said, it's a wonderful thing to have a goal like this for yourself. No matter how old you are, no matter where you live.

NOTES

On Literary Prizes

1. *Selected Letters of Raymond Chandler,* ed. Frank MacShane (New York: Columbia University Press, 1981), 180–1.
2. As quoted in Studs Terkel with Sydney Lewis, *Touch and Go: A Memoir* (New York: The New Press, 2007), 197.

On Originality

1. Oliver Sacks, "Prodigies," in *An Anthropologist on Mars: Seven Paradoxical Tales* (New York: Vintage, 1996), 241–2.
2. As quoted in Robert Harris, *Aphorism* (Tokyo: Sanctuary Press), 2010.

A Note About the Author

Haruki Murakami was born in Kyoto in 1949 and now lives near Tokyo. His work has been translated into more than fifty languages, and the most recent of his many international honors is the Hans Christian Andersen Literature Award, whose other recipients include Karl Ove Knausgård, Isabel Allende, and Salman Rushdie.

A Note on the Type

This book was set in a typeface named Bulmer. This distinguished letter is a replica of a type long famous in the history of English printing that was designed and cut by William Martin in about 1790 for William Bulmer of the Shakespeare Press. In design, it is all but a modern face, with vertical stress, sharp differentiation between the thick and thin strokes, and nearly flat serifs. The decorative italic shows the influence of Baskerville, as Martin was a pupil of John Baskerville's.

Composed by North Market Street Graphics, Lancaster, Pennsylvania
Printed and bound by Berryville Graphics, Berryville, Virginia
Designed by Anna B. Knighton and Chip Kidd